estherpress

Books for Courageous Women

ESTHER PRESS VISION

Publishing diverse voices that encourage and equip women to walk courageously in the light of God's truth for such a time as this.

BIBLICAL STATEMENT OF PURPOSE

"For if you keep silent at this time, relief and deliverance will rise for the Jews from another place, but you and your father's house will perish. And who knows whether you have not come to the kingdom for such a time as this?"

Esther 4:14 (ESV)

What people are saying about …

PRAY WITH ME

"How I wish I'd had this book as a young mom! *Pray with Me* provides creative ways to take prayer off the fine china shelf and place it directly into the hands of your children. You'll discover a toolbox of ideas to not only equip your children to have meaningful and genuine conversations with God but to also bring Jesus into their everyday lives. Through Scripture, biblical wisdom, personal stories, and simply worded scripts, Erica provides foundational principles you can build on year after year to keep your children engaged with God, even through the challenging teenage years."

Wendy Blight, author, biblical content specialist
for Proverbs 31 Ministries online Bible studies

"A common cry among children's and youth ministry workers is that the parents are a child's most important spiritual influence but not enough is done to equip them. With numerous practical and biblical examples and personal stories, Erica equips! She provides numerous go-to ministry tools for influencing our children to talk to God. So get the book, start reading—and pray with your kids in fresh and meaningful ways!"

Jim Jackson, cofounder of Connected Families, speaker,
and coauthor of *How to Grow a Connected Family* and
Discipline That Connects with Your Child's Heart

"Raw. Real. Road-tested. *Pray with Me* is a dynamic toolkit for partnering with God to help nurture little disciples whom God will grow into giants of faith. What a gift for all who long for the children they love to experience God personally!"

Dr. Rex Keener, senior pastor, Grace
Fellowship, Albany, New York

"It's difficult to find someone as likeable and approachable as Erica. She's simply what she appears to be—with no pretense or disguise. If she has messed up, she'll own it and, with raw honesty, tell you what she's learned from it. If she's found success, she'll excitedly give you the recipe without bragging. This book invites you in, offers you a comfortable seat, and pours you a warm cup of honesty and hope."

Homer Purdy, operations director,
ALIVE Radio Network

"In *Pray with Me*, Erica's precepts are pragmatic without being dogmatic. The book is written tenderly as a guide, filled with both biblical insight and kitchen table encouragement. While *Pray with Me* is written to teach children to pray, there is also plenty of insight to fuel the hearts of parents (and grandparents) as well."

Ronne Rock, teacher, mentor, author of
One Woman Can Change the World

ERICA RENAUD

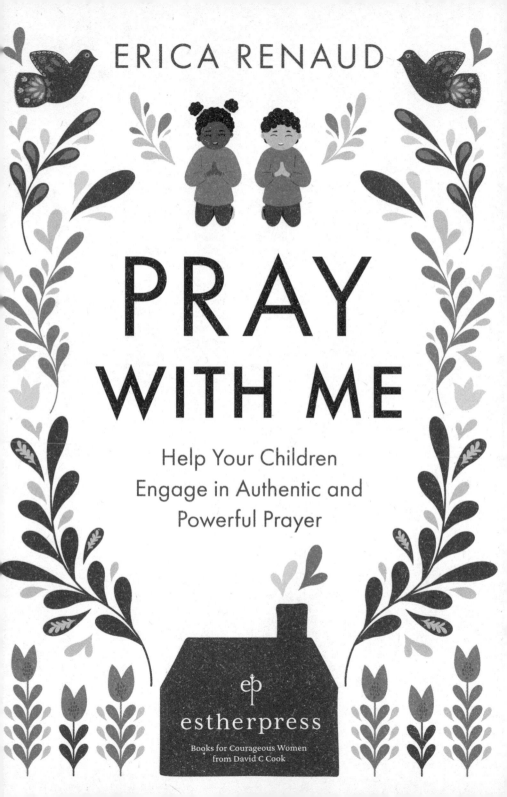

PRAY
WITH ME

Help Your Children
Engage in Authentic and
Powerful Prayer

estherpress

Books for Courageous Women
from David C Cook

PRAY WITH ME
Published by Esther Press,
an imprint of David C Cook
4050 Lee Vance Drive
Colorado Springs, CO 80918 U.S.A.

Integrity Music Limited, a Division of David C Cook
Brighton, East Sussex BN1 2RE, England

Esther Press, David C Cook, and related logos are trademarks of David C Cook.

The website addresses recommended throughout this book are offered as a
resource to you. These websites are not intended in any way to be or imply an
endorsement on the part of David C Cook, nor do we vouch for their content.

Unless otherwise noted, all Scripture quotations are taken from the Christian
Standard Bible®, Copyright © 2017 by Holman Bible Publishers. Used by
permission. Christian Standard Bible® and CSB® are federally registered
trademarks of Holman Bible Publishers. Scripture quotations marked ESV
are taken from the ESV® Bible (The Holy Bible, English Standard Version®),
copyright © 2001 by Crossway, a publishing ministry of Good News Publishers.
Used by permission. All rights reserved; NIV are taken from the Holy Bible,
New International Version®, NIV®. Copyright © 1973, 2011 by Biblica, Inc.™
Used by permission of Zondervan. All rights reserved worldwide. www.
zondervan.com. The "NIV" and "New International Version" are trademarks
registered in the United States Patent and Trademark Office by Biblica, Inc.™
The author has added italics to Scripture quotations for emphasis.

Library of Congress Control Number 2022944339
ISBN 978-0-8307-8452-3
eISBN 978-0-8307-8453-0

The Team: Susan McPherson, Stephanie Bennett, Judy Gillispie,
Karissa Silvers, James Hershberger, Susan Murdock
Cover Design: Emily Weigel
Cover Illustrations: © Chus Moreno Studio/
CreativeMarket and © N.Savranska/Shutterstock

Printed in the United States of America
First Edition 2023

1 2 3 4 5 6 7 8 9 10

120822

Dedicated to Kaylee, Lucy, Mariele, Josiah, and Malachi. May the Lord's face be more glorious to you than anything this earth has to offer.

And to Mom, for teaching me how to look into Jesus' face when I pray.

CONTENTS

FOREWORD

Train up a child in the way he should go, and
when he is old he will not depart from it.

Proverbs 22:6

If you're anything like me, when you read the first few words, "Train up a child in the way he should go," you begin to feel overwhelmed. You think of all that's involved in raising a child in twenty-first century America, as well as the implications of the verse in regard to the formation of their faith and spirituality. You break out in a sweat. Life can get busy, complex at times; being a parent is challenging and often exhausting. And as a parent, I have often said to myself, "There's not much apparent about being a parent."

As I consider the rest of the proverb for the wisdom it contains, I cling to what I believe to be great hope for parents from God: "and when he is old he will not depart from it." I believe that this proverb is God's Word for us, containing encouragement that we must cling to as we consider the overwhelming nature of parenting today. This proverb recognizes that our work as parents is that of co-laborers with God in His sovereign plan to bring salvation to our children. This is the daily privilege of parenting!

Erica Renaud is on to something here as she writes to encourage parents to nurture their children in faith, to pray with them, and to teach them to pray. Our desire to nurture our children in a lifestyle of eternal communion with God is linked to our passionate hope for their salvation. As you read this book, you will be drawn to Erica's insights and practical applications. You will be captivated by her stories. You will be encouraged by her blatant honesty. You will be inspired by her passion.

In *Praying Circles around Your Children*, Mark Batterson writes, "Praying for your kids is like taking them for a ride; praying with your kids is like teaching them to drive. If all you ever do is pray for your kids, they'll just stay in the backseat. Your kids will become spiritual codependents who ask you for a ride anytime they need to get somewhere spiritually. But if you teach them to pray, they can download directions themselves and make their way to wherever it is that God wants them to go."

So I encourage you to read Erica's book with excitement. But before you begin, there are a few things I would like to share with you. You probably don't know Erica like I do, so I want to tell you a little about her. I believe if you know a few vital things, you will be captured by her words all the more.

I met Erica when she was a teenager and a single mom. She was courted by and later engaged to Jesse Renaud, my assistant pastor. For a number of years, I was a pastor to Erica and Jesse while they were living in southern New Jersey. I saw them come together as young adults and fall deeply in love. They stood in front of me and exchanged marriage vows. I led them as they dedicated their children to God. We also shared life together as disciples of Jesus—praying regularly, worshipping, and doing ministry together. So I know Erica very well. In fact, as I read through *Pray With Me*, I can hear Erica's voice and visualize her interactions with her husband and children in each story. What I want you to know is that she writes of her reality; it's all true day-to-day stuff. It's who she is. It's her life.

Erica grew up in a home with parents who loved Jesus and desired to instill their faith in their children. They did everything they could to nurture her in faith. They took her and her siblings to church, and they prayed with them at home. They helped their children flesh out their faith as they grew. Yet, as Erica tells us, following Jesus was not always easy for her. There were times when she stumbled in her walk with Christ. These times drove her to her knees, to discover a deeper abiding presence of her Lord and Savior. These experiences helped her embrace God's love and forgiveness and grow in His grace.

As Erica writes in these pages, she shares her life and her faith. She shares her communion with God and invites you into that experience. Erica is on to something here, and my prayer is that as you read these pages, the Holy Spirit will enlighten you, challenge you, encourage you, and inspire you to move toward a deeper communion with God and to take your children with you.

Forward for Jesus and His church,

Rev. Dr. Jamie Bagley
Carll's Corner Community Fellowship
Bridgeton, NJ

LETTER TO MOTHERS

From Erica Renaud

Hey, Mama,

I see you standing there, holding this book and excited to read it. But having just looked at the thickness of it and skimmed the table of contents, you're probably also wondering if you'll actually have time to sit down and get through it all, let alone implement what I'm suggesting here. I get it. I've been there!

I wonder if the Israelites felt the same way after Moses recited the lengthy and detailed law to them. I can imagine the sarcastic mom in the back, bouncing her baby on her hip, nudging her friend, and making a face that says, *Yeah, right. Who's going to do all that?*

But when Moses was done, he said something really interesting:

> This command that I give you today is certainly not too difficult or beyond your reach. It is not in heaven so that you have to ask, "Who will go up to heaven, get it for us, and proclaim it to us so that we may follow it?" … *But the message is very near you, in your mouth and in your heart, so that you may follow it.* (Deut. 30:11–12, 14)

Lean in a little. The suggestions I'm making in this book are not some lofty standards for you to someday reach. All the information and ideas you hold in your hands are meant to help you implement the desire that is *already in your heart*: to raise your children in prayer.

In the course of reading this book, I hope you'll see that praying with our children is not some unattainable goal. You know why?

Because God is close.

He's there, in the middle of the tantrum and the crying over the skinned knee. He couldn't be closer when sadness over a loved one's death sweeps through the house. He's right with us when we're overwhelmed, frustrated, and disappointed. God is so near to us and our children. It is my prayer that this book will act as a catalyst for shifting first our hearts and then our children's hearts, allowing us to see and connect with God in everything we do.

> Jesus, thank You for this mother's heart for her children. Would You bless her and her children tremendously? Give her grace to come alongside her little ones and pray. Give her a tender and discerning heart to know how to lead them well. May she begin to see You in all the little crevices of life.
>
> In Jesus' mighty name, amen.

LETTER TO FATHERS

From Jesse Renaud

My most vivid memory from my fifth year of life is sitting on my father's lap to pray. We had just heard the gospel shared at vacation Bible school. My twin brother sat beside me as I asked Jesus to forgive and save me.

Dads, you probably already know this if you're picking up this book, but I'll remind you anyway: your role in your child's life is crucial. It is no accident that God refers to Himself as Father over and over again in the Scriptures. We as fathers have a singularly unique role in representing God to our children and leading them to Him. No pressure, right?

I've always been particularly convicted by Ephesians 6:4, which says, "Fathers, do not provoke your children to anger, but bring them up in the discipline and instruction of the Lord" (ESV). I thought "not provok[ing] my children to anger" would be easy until I started having them! So the beginning part of that verse alone is a challenge, but the second half gets even weightier: "bring them up in the discipline and instruction of the Lord."

As arduous as this verse seems, I've come to believe that *praying with our children* might just be the very best way to work toward accomplishing both parts of this verse. When we make praying with our kids a regular practice, it's much harder to be impatient with them. Additionally, I can't think of a more impactful way to "discipline and instruct" our children in the Lord than by teaching them to pray. We model something priceless when we come before our heavenly Father in reverence, awe, dependency, and authenticity.

So pray with your kids, in all kinds of ways and in all kinds of situations. Pray with them at the dinner table and their bedside, for little things and big things. Pray at all times—in good times, bad times, and everything in between. I know from personal experience that you will see God do amazing things—in both you and your children!

Our God and Father, You know the heart of the father holding this book. You know everything about him—his joys, his passions, his faults, and his weaknesses—and yet You love him. Not only that, but You also take delight in him!

Give this father the humility to come before You with reverence and awe. May he not hold anything back but trust in Your power and sovereignty over everything, especially his family. Give him the grace he needs to pray and the patience to draw his children in as he does. May he teach them by example, modeling what it means to trust You, depend on You, and experience that You are who You say You are.

In Jesus' great name, amen.

LETTER TO CHILDREN'S MINISTRY WORKERS

If you work in kids' ministry, I commend you. It may feel at times that people see you as a babysitter, and perhaps some do, but God doesn't. You are helping to disciple small souls. You are shepherding eternal beings—with your smile, your tenderheartedness, your teaching, and your love.

When I worked in children's ministry, I always wanted the parents to be on board. My hope was that they would reinforce the ideas we were teaching on Sunday. We saw the children for only one day each week, but we desperately wanted to impact the rest of their week.

Unfortunately, I never had much success with that. I had handouts and crafts; I even stood at the door and gave each parent a quick summary of what we learned that day. (People at the end of the pickup line didn't *love* that.)

I eventually thought, *If parents are teaching their kids at home, then great! What does it matter if we're on the same page?* After that, I began to notice all the kids coming whose parents *weren't* teaching them at home. Maybe a grandma, a stepparent, or some-one else brought them because their parents didn't go to church.

My mission became clear—I wanted the kids to experience God, if only for a brief moment, whether through worship, teaching, or prayer. I just wanted them to get a small taste of His love.

I pray this book encourages you to help children experience God. While I've written this book primarily with parents in mind, many of these ideas came out of my time in the classroom. The majority of the suggestions can be used as is or altered slightly to fit the classroom. Let's bring prayer into our teaching time so children can taste for themselves how great God is!

> Jesus, thank You for the children's ministry worker reading this. Thank You that they see something most people miss: Your great love for children.
>
> I pray for their heart, that they would see children the way You do. Give them ears to hear what You have to say about the children they teach. May You open their mouth to speak prophetic words of encouragement straight to the children's hearts.
>
> May this teacher spend so much time in Your presence that their face would shine like Moses's did as it reflects Your glory. When children see their smile and hear their voice, may they get a glimpse of Your goodness.
>
> In Jesus' mighty name, amen.

 Introduction

LET THE CHILDREN COME

If I could pay a million dollars to guarantee that my children would have a deep and lasting relationship with Jesus, believe me, I would find a way! My hunch is I'm not alone here. I've yet to meet a Christian parent who didn't desire for their children to share in their faith. It is, of course, a parent's greatest joy and ultimate goal to see their children walk with Christ in faith and live their lives for Him.

I didn't take anything seriously before I had children. Grades? *Good grades are for nerds.* College? *Eh, overrated.* Career? *Americans are too career obsessed.* Life was just a big adventure, but the moment my daughter was born, I started to take everything seriously. Well, that is, after the laughing gas from my c-section wore off.

To be fair, I was only eighteen when my daughter was born, so that may have been the reason I didn't have a five-year plan or 401(k). Even so, I'm pretty sure that I could've been president at the time and I still would've said that everything I accomplished prior to her birth was utterly meaningless.

When your child is born, there's a sobering sense that nothing in your life mattered before that moment. We know this is not really true, but having children does change everything—our outlook, our goals, our perspective, our role, our plans, even our faith.

A unique heaviness accompanies parenthood. At eighteen, this hit me especially hard. It is the weight of knowing that you are now fully responsible for another human being, that you are to take care of not only their physical needs but their emotional, mental, and spiritual needs as well. See, we are not just raising people; we are raising eternal beings. We are raising souls.

Years ago, an older and wiser friend told my new hubby and me that we needed to decide for ourselves what it meant to be successful. We talked it through, but there wasn't much to discuss; we were in total agreement. Success for us meant raising our children to know and love Jesus. We went a step further and thought of people we believed had done this well and what it was about them or the way they parented that seemed to be different.

Right from the start, we parented our children with a mission and a purpose—teaching, praying, and loving the best we could. We kept Sunday service a priority, we taught about God at opportune times, and we prayed before bed and after boo-boos. There was only one issue, one uncomfortable truth looming in the background of everything we did: no matter how well we did as parents, we were not in control of their faith. God was. No matter what I did, I could not guarantee any outcomes regarding my children's happiness, health, marriage, career, *or* faith.

Marty Machowski, a family pastor and author said, "There is no slam dunk in parenting." This truth was hard to hear as a young mom who threw herself into motherhood the way most people in their early twenties throw themselves into college and career. *Surely if I did the right things and taught the right things, my children would be happy, healthy adults with a strong faith in Jesus?* I hoped. *Surely, there was a secret, a checklist, or a level of intentionality that would ensure a solid future for my children?*

Our goal, then, is not for our children to know *about* Jesus but to know *Him.*

If you are hoping this book is your ticket to guarantee a certain future for your children, I'll save you the time and tell you right now that it's not. But no book is. No strategy, methodology, or level of diligence and intentionality will guarantee your children turn out "right."

The truth is, our children don't get to heaven by *our* sweat and tears; they get there by *Jesus'* blood. I cannot give you a slam dunk method. But what I can do is show you how we can come alongside our children and point them to Jesus in prayer. I can show you how we as parents can lay the foundation for prayer when our children are young so they will have something to build on as they mature and grow. I can show you how our children can have a rich relationship with Jesus through prayer.

See, all the facts and information we pass on to our children will fall flat if they don't have a relationship with Christ. Our goal, then, is not for our children to know *about* Jesus but to know *Him*.

I started out thinking this book was about equipping parents to lead their children in prayer so that kids could know Jesus for themselves. And it absolutely is. But I've discovered it's also about raising children to be active and discerning members of the body of Christ who are awake, aware, and in tune with the voice of God in a culture that is moving further away from Him.

Matthew 19:13 says, "Children were brought to Jesus." Notice it doesn't even say *who* brought these children. It doesn't matter. What is important is what they *did*—they brought children to Jesus.

That heavy weight of feeling like it's all up to us is an unnecessary burden. Jesus is ready to prove Himself. Jesus is pursuing our children. Jesus is welcoming them. Whether we are moms, dads, grandparents, nannies, or teachers, our role is simple.

Jesus said, "Let the little children come" (v. 14 ESV).

All we have to do is bring them.

 Chapter 1

THE GREATEST INHERITANCE

My relationship with Jesus began with a prayer. I was eight.

While reading a Precious Moments storybook Bible, I came to a page in between stories that explained salvation. It invited the reader to pray and receive Christ. I prayed along with that prayer and put my faith in Jesus for the first time. I was alone in my room. No one told me to, no one asked me to, and I'm not sure my parents even knew an invitation like that was in my Bible. It was just a special moment between God and me.

I genuinely desired to follow Him after that. I remember praying for my classmates in my spiral journal, praying with my mom when she came and sat on my bed, and praying along with my father's genuine prayers of gratitude at dinnertime. However, that pure desire took a hit when I entered high school. Outwardly, I looked like a typical rebellious teen. I had poor grades, ran away twice, and went through a twelve-step program. I wasn't traveling the "straight and narrow path" Christian parents hope their children will walk on.

Sometime in my late twenties, I came across several journals I'd kept in high school. These journals held records from my days, as well as the prayers of my heart. Reading through them reminded me what was going on *within* me during that time.

As if the emotions that come with adolescent years weren't enough, my heart was in a constant struggle. My wholehearted desire to live for God began to divide as I discovered the plethora of temptations the world was dishing out.

I was like Christian entering the city of Vanity Fair in John Bunyan's *The Pilgrim's Progress*. If you've never read the book, it's an allegorical story of the journey we take as believers. Only in Bunyan's story, the main character, Christian, resisted all the shiny temptations meant to lure travelers away from their true mission. That was not the case with me. Instead, a war raged within me: my sin nature versus my heart for God. I desired both the straight-and-narrow path and the streets of Vegas.

After letting my sin nature take the reins for a time, I'd eventually repent "for real." I'd go a few months keeping my focus on God, but inevitably I would fall back into the same destructive sin. I went through this cycle repeatedly. I repented so often, I hardly believed myself.

A follower of Christ cannot follow both the world and Christ for long before the tension mounts within them and something must give. Feeling trapped in this cycle, I figured it would be easier to endure if I stopped caring. I became apathetic. I did the church things but cared little, and I did the destructive things with a numb conscience.

By my senior year, I believed that my only hope for lasting change was to fail completely and devastatingly. One night I told a couple of my closest friends, "I think I may have to hit rock bottom in order to be done with this and finally come up for good." In my naivety, I had no idea just how far from rock bottom I was, but that statement exemplified the weight of helplessness I felt.

Despite my attempts at apathy, I repeatedly prayed, "Lord, change me, because I cannot change myself." Thankfully, God's hand of grace did change me, and the only rock I hit was Him.

I thought I would need to run my life into the ground in order to change, but God used something—actually, someone—beautiful and precious instead. Toward the end of my senior year, I discovered I was pregnant.

It was during my pregnancy that many things shifted for me. Physically, of course, but spiritually as well. Things that once seemed so alluring became meaningless and shallow. I was finally able to let go of the temptations that repeatedly lured me away and seek God with a renewed sense of freedom.

While outwardly I looked like a typical rebellious teen, inwardly I was crying out to God for help the only way I knew how—through prayer. Later, as I looked through the pages of my journals, I was confronted with prayer after prayer begging God to intervene. Even in my "rebellion" I hadn't stopped seeking Him.

Why did I turn back to Him over and over again? Why didn't I just forget God so I could do what I wanted? Why couldn't I just walk away?

I'm sure the influence of my parents, quality friends, and youth leaders all helped. I'm sure going to youth group and church on Sunday helped too. But as I flipped through page after page, one thing became clear: by high school I had already established something very powerful with God—a relationship.

The Importance of a Relationship

Aside from when I prayed to receive Christ at age eight, the majority of my prayer life looked pretty mundane. Yet, like the roots of a tree, all these little moments with God grew and strengthened my relationship with Him. Jeremiah 17:7–8 compares someone who trusts in God to a tree. It reads:

> The person who trusts in the LORD,
> whose confidence indeed is the LORD, is blessed.
>
> He will be like a tree planted by water:
> it sends its roots out toward a stream,
> it doesn't fear when heat comes,
> and its foliage remains green.
> It will not worry in a year of drought
> or cease producing fruit.

Jeremiah says that one who trusts in the Lord is like this mighty tree that can handle the harsh elements of nature and various seasons and trials. But this kind of trust doesn't happen overnight. Trust in God, like trust in anyone, requires time and is developed through intentionality.

My high school years were far from the model of unwavering trust in God that Jeremiah talks about. But they do model the power of a relationship with God. Despite my attempts to ignore His tug on my heart so I could do as I pleased, I couldn't actually walk away. That relationship kept me tethered to Him when I was tempted to turn and go down my own path.

And at the center of that relationship was prayer. It was through prayer that my relationship with Him began. It was through prayer that I sought His help. It was through prayer that I wrestled with the desires of my heart. It was through prayer that I confessed my sins to God and He renewed me over and over again. It was in simply talking with Him that His Spirit encouraged me.

Storms Ahead

It's nerve-racking when the generation after us begins driving. Besides feeling old, part of us feels like, "No way are they ready for that!" That was the case with my nephew. I had seen him as a baby, as a toddler, then as a rambunctious little boy. I thought, *He's tall, but he's barely older than a child. No way he's old enough to drive!* Yet he was, by law anyway. And to his credit, he's done an excellent job.

Seeing him begin to drive got me thinking about my own daughter, who's a little younger than him. I began to worry and wondered what kinds of problems or issues she might run into.

As parents, we ask similar questions when trying to prepare our children for life. Especially when we see something that goes majorly wrong for someone else, we can't help but think, *What can I do to keep* that *from happening?* When reflecting on my own high school years, I've often thought, *Gosh, how can I prevent that from happening to my kids?*

It's natural to want to prevent our children from encountering hardship. I think it's part of our parental nature to want to protect. But notice that God doesn't keep the tree in Jeremiah from experiencing tough circumstances. In fact, as was the case with my high school years, God oftentimes uses storms to strengthen our relationship with Him.

 What better way to prepare our children for storms than to introduce them to the One who calms them?

After my nephew had been driving a bit and was ready to buy his first car, my dad got him a gift. Instead of stressing and trying to prevent things from going wrong, he took a different approach. He thought ahead to what might solve the problems my nephew would definitely face and got him a bag. The bag contained a car-battery charger, road flares, a blanket, a flashlight, emergency food, and a whole bunch of other necessities, along with the understanding that no matter what happened, my nephew could always call Grandpa Tom for help.

If we want our children to have a strong and resilient faith that can weather the trials they will face throughout their lifetime, we must stop trying to prevent storms and start preparing for them. During the time I've been writing this book, I've heard news stories about civil wars, uprisings, and turmoil in various countries, as well as the persecution of Christians in all parts of the globe. After reading an article about the unrest in yet another country, I couldn't help but think, *If we heard bombs going off each night and knew the imminent threat of being hit, captured, or separated, how might I talk to my children about Jesus and about prayer? What would prayer look like if that were our situation?*

I want to seek Him with that kind of urgency. I want my children to trust Him like their lives depend on it. Because they do. The stable country we live in, the homes we reside in, the lovely future we anticipate—these things can sometimes act as a facade, masking the truth that each and every breath we breathe is from God. The only one we can truly count on is Him. The only thing that is truly stable and unchanging is God.

And what better way to prepare our children for storms than to introduce them to the One who calms them? As we think through the trials they might encounter, the conflicts they might face, the wars they might live through, the organizations they might stand up to, the pain they might endure, the most valuable thing we could ever do for our children is to bring them to Jesus—the only One who can sustain them through the storm, deliver them out of it, and make them stronger because of it!

Our Role as Parents

Prayer continued to strengthen my relationship with God, and not only did it keep me tethered to Him during my teen years, but it also became the way I leaned on Him wholeheartedly through a variety of challenges that accompanied adulthood.

A year and a half after my daughter was born, I married a guitar-playing, theology-loving man of God. We moved into a tiny apartment in New Jersey, where we quickly began adding to our family. We added another daughter, and then another. Three girls in all. During our time in that apartment, we struggled financially. We took turns taking classes at the local college and juggled multiple jobs and lots of diapers.

One evening, my husband and I once again looked at our financial situation, trying to determine how long it would be until things might change. But nothing looked promising. In the end, we concluded that our best opportunity for change would come after my husband finished school in another two years. When you're living day to day, two years seems dreadfully far away.

We had already been living off so little, and now even looking ahead didn't help. It actually did just the opposite. Our talk was intended to be like climbing to higher ground to gain a better view of our future. But instead of bringing relief and the sight of a brighter path, it brought despair as we looked out and saw more of the same hardship.

I cried out to God that evening. "How can we build a family with no money? Money functions like … the foundation for a family!" Even as I said those words, I knew I was wrong, but with nothing but raw frustration, I couldn't see what was right either. God didn't delay in responding, *"No, I am your foundation."* At His words, all the struggles, frugal living, hand-me-downs, and ramen noodles that seemed to define our life—and now our future—crumbled. And I could see what was really happening. All the difficulties we were experiencing were strengthening our faith, our trust, and our complete and utter dependence on God. And He never failed us. He held us, led us, and provided for us repeatedly.

As a mother, I want my children to know this God. As a parent who wants a good and bright future for my kids, I desperately want them to *know this Jesus*—the One who never leaves us, never forsakes us, and never abandons us but walks with us through all life's difficulties and guides us through all life's storms. I pray regularly that my children will know *this* God.

I would think that of all the things we parents place importance on, our children's relationship with God would be top of the list. But I was shocked recently to discover that according to a Barna Group survey, only three out of ten Christian parents considered the salvation of their children a priority. The number one answer given was a good education.[1] While our kids' education can certainly influence their future, I doubt that parents will be patting themselves on the back in eternity saying, "I'm so glad our Johnny got a good education!"

I'm going to assume that if you're reading this book, the salvation of your children is a priority and you see it as your responsibility to raise them in the faith and share the good news with them.

Regardless of what we look to as affirmation of our children's salvation, our job isn't done if or when they make a decision to follow Jesus. First, it seems pretty clear from Matthew that when Jesus returns, there will be many who *expect* to enter into His kingdom but *won't*:

> On that day *many* will say to me, "Lord, Lord, didn't we prophesy in your name, drive out demons in your name, and do many miracles in your name?"

Then I will announce to them, "I never knew you.
Depart from me...." (Matt. 7:22–23)

There will be people who profess belief in Jesus and do works
and even miracles in His name who think they are Christians but
who don't actually know Him, nor does He know them. I think
we should be very hesitant to *assume* our children are saved. I
don't know about you, but when Jesus returns in all His glory,
I don't want my children thinking they will be welcomed into
God's kingdom only to be turned away. I wonder if this is part of
the reason why Revelation says,

Look, he is coming with the clouds,
and every eye will see him,
even those who pierced him.
And all the tribes of the earth
will mourn over him.
So it is to be. Amen. (1:7)

That day Jesus returns will be glorious and magnificent but
also terrifying and sobering. Face to face with His perfection and
holiness, everyone will see themselves clearly, and *many* will realize they are not what they thought.

Second, why wait for visible evidence that our children are
saved before we teach them to pray? While some in the Bible
had a clear and dramatic conversion experience, not everyone
did. In fact, we don't really know when the majority of the disciples had a saving faith. And yet, it seems almost certain that

their relationship with Jesus and trust in Him grew before that point. Because of this, I don't think we should wait to teach our children how to pray until they've made some kind of profession of faith.

Talking about children, Jesus said, "See to it that you don't despise one of these little ones, because I tell you that in heaven their angels continually view the face of my Father in heaven" (Matt. 18:10). If children have angels who are speaking to God each day on their behalf, I'm not going to deny them the opportunity to talk to God themselves.

Last, suppose we can and do feel sure our children are saved, then what? Is that the end? Have we completed our assignment? No, not at all. Our children's faith still needs to grow. Their salvation still needs to be worked out (see Phil. 2:12). Let's look at what Deuteronomy says our job is: "*Love* the LORD your God with all your heart, with all your soul, and with all your strength. These words that I am giving you today are to be in your heart. Repeat them to your children" (6:5–7a). Our role can be summed up like this: love God intensely and teach our children to do the same. How could we possibly love God without prayer? Likewise, how could we teach our children to love God without showing them how to pray?

Our job as parents is not to "get our children saved." It's to teach our children *how we love God*. It's to disciple them into a genuine relationship with Him, where they depend on Him, trust Him, and live for Him alone. If we never teach them to pray, we miss the whole point of salvation—to know Jesus and have a loving relationship with Him.

Knowing God for Themselves

Not only did God provide for my family financially while we lived in that apartment, but we also had an enriching friend group and a church family that greatly encouraged our faith. It was in this season that I began praying in ways I never had before. I began interceding on a regular basis for my children, my church, and my city. I learned how to read the Bible and use it to fuel my prayers. And I discovered how to pray for others, beginning by listening to God's heart for them. My relationship with God that began as a child and was tested in my teen years was now becoming solid as God continued to reveal Himself. It felt like I was swimming in deep water for the first time and everything before that had just been splashing around.

It was in that season that I partnered with a friend, and together we led the children's ministry at our church. We talked and prayed regularly about the direction we were heading and what we wanted to teach the children next. I loved our conversations. We both had powerful testimonies of experiencing God in our lives, so the question that was constantly in the front of our minds was, *How can we help the children know this God for themselves?*

Our hope was to teach about God in such a way that they wouldn't just take our word for it but seek Him on their own. We continued in solid teaching so they would know His Word and His character, but we tried to teach in a way that welcomed them into a relationship with this God of the Bible. We added to that lots of teaching on prayer and allowed time for prayer in the classroom. Our goals became simple: give the children solid teaching about God, a chance to experience God through prayer, and tools to seek Him *on their own.*

Take My Word for It

As Christian parents, we can feel especially anxious for our children to share our beliefs. Although we may want our children to take our word for it on most matters, if this is our approach to teaching them about God, we will be shortchanging God by not giving Him the opportunity to prove Himself! Of course, we cannot truly limit God, but we are doing a huge disservice to our children if we don't point them directly to God so they can see and know Him for themselves.

Over and over the Bible reveals that God's desire is to be *known* and *experienced* by His people. While we all think of the exodus as a sign of God's great love for His people—and it is—it's also a giant expression of His desire to be truly known by His people. In describing the events that would take place during the exodus, God repeatedly used phrases about being known: "so that you may know there is no one like the LORD our God" (Ex. 8:10), "and you will know that I am the LORD" (10:2), "and the Egyptians will know that I am the LORD" (14:4). In fact, before the plagues even began, God told Moses what He was going to do and *why*: "I will take you as my people, and I will be your God. You will know that I am the LORD your God, who brought you out from the forced labor of the Egyptians" (6:7).

After David escaped the hands of King Abimelech, he praised God and said, "Taste and see that the LORD is good" (Ps. 34:8). In other words, "Look, don't just take my word for it; you can experience Him too! You can know His goodness too!"

This was not the first time David had experienced God's hand, though. Sunday school teachers and parents of young children all love the story of the young shepherd boy David defeating the Philistine giant, Goliath. Somehow this twiggy boy had enough courage to stand up to a trained soldier many times his size.

While this is definitely an encouraging story of how God can use children, that's not the part of the story that moves my heart most. Before David fought Goliath, Saul had David brought to him and said, "You can't go fight this Philistine. You're just a youth, and he's been a warrior since he was young" (1 Sam. 17:33).

Saul made a good point. What grounds did David have to be confident? So what was David's reply?

David went on to reveal that while everyone thought he was just a lazy shepherd boy, he had actually been fighting off lions and bears!

> Your servant has been tending his father's sheep.
> Whenever a lion or a bear came and carried off a
> lamb from the flock, I went after it, struck it down,
> and rescued the lamb from its mouth. If it reared
> up against me, I would grab it by its fur, strike it
> down, and kill it. (vv. 34–35)

I imagine that everyone in that room must have looked at him the same way a group of young people in their twenties looked at my seven-year-old son recently when he stepped out on the dance floor and started break dancing at a wedding. "Wait, what?! Who is this kid?"

While anyone else might've used this as an opportunity to brag about their own strength, David knew it was God who had allowed him to fight off those wild animals. He said, "The LORD who rescued me from the paw of the lion and the paw of the bear will rescue me from the hand of this Philistine" (v. 37).

Because of his experience with God, David had confidence that God would help him defeat the Philistine even though he was many times larger than David. David wasn't intimidated while everyone else was cowering because, compared with God's strength, Goliath seemed small!

Do you see? God doesn't just *use* children; He does much more than that. God *reveals* Himself to children so they might *know* Him and walk *confidently* with Him.

If our goal is to pass on information and get our children to just say a prayer, then we'll only manage to teach them a religion. We won't actually introduce them to the One who formed them in their mother's womb, who has counted the hairs on their head, who hears their every thought and knows their every desire, who seeks them out and who calls them by name!

God has assignments for our children. God has plans for our children. God has places for them and roles for them. Who knows what God wants to do through our children or in what ways He wants to use them in His kingdom? What we can be certain of is that God is not content for them to know cute stories about Him; He wants them to *know* Him.

When we teach our children to talk with God and listen for His voice, they will see for *themselves* that God is who He says He is. And this is far more powerful than simply taking our word for it.

Back to the Tree

What makes a tree beautiful anyway? Is it its size or shape, its branches or blossoms? All these things contribute to the tree's beauty, for sure. But the part of the tree that is most responsible for its beauty is actually its roots. Ironically, no one will ever walk up to a beautiful tree and compliment its roots. Roots are hidden, pale, and dirty. But without them, there would be no outward beauty.

Prayer functions like the roots of a tree. As we pray with our children, we are helping them develop strong and deep roots. When we choose to pause and pray, when we make prayer a priority, we help deepen our children's dependence on Jesus and grow their roots in Him. But like the roots of a tree, prayer won't always feel glorious. It may seem rather lackluster, rote, or even boring.

 In a time when everyone is doing everything they can to be seen, I believe God is calling us as parents to seek the hidden things.

Similarly, no one is going to compliment you on praying with your children. No one is going to praise you for it. Likely, no one will even notice.

So here's my challenge. In a time when everyone is doing everything they can to be seen, I believe God is calling us as parents to seek the hidden things. To seek God in prayer and to begin praying with our children. To invite them into those special moments, bringing them alongside us to seek God together, turning to Him first and foremost. Not for anyone else, for praise, or for glory, but simply because we can't think of a greater inheritance we could possibly pass on to our children than to help them find Jesus and *know* Him.

> Jesus, You know the plans You have for each of my children. You know the trials they will face and the storms they will weather. Give me grace to bring my children to You. I pray that like David, they would experience Your goodness and say, "Taste and see that the LORD is good!"

Chapter 2

MAYBE THEY'LL GET IT WHEN THEY'RE OLDER

Everyone shifted and squeezed so we could all fit at the dinner table. Around it sat myself, my husband, our five children, and my parents, who we were living with at the time. After waiting for the commotion to settle, my husband asked our oldest son, who was barely three, if he wanted to pray. My son was a late talker and struggled to enunciate words. We understood a decent amount of what he said, but few others could.

Sitting around hot plates of food, we all closed our eyes. My husband led the prayer, leaving a pause so my son could repeat after him: "God." My son followed along: "God." "Thank You for this food." "Thank You for this food." "Help us to love You." "Help us to love You." "And help us to love each other." My son went rogue: "And help me to not fall off my bike."

Remember in *How the Grinch Stole Christmas!* when the Grinch's heart gets bigger and bigger till it can't get any bigger? It felt as though my heart could not possibly get any bigger at that moment. My son had been learning to ride his bike that day and had already fallen quite a few times. Now, here around a tableful of people, he prayed earnestly for God to help him stay on his bike. From his vantage point, I guess he felt that not falling was more important than loving others.

I believe this was one of the first prayers he prayed on his own. Prior to this moment, he'd only repeated prayers his father or I had led. This was his first time expressing to God the desires in *his* heart.

I'm sure we'd talked about God, and he had certainly seen us pray, but I have no recollection of specifically explaining what prayer was. Regardless, he had clearly received all the "instruction" he needed. At the very least, he picked up on the fact that we can ask God for things. And being that he was very aware of his desire not to fall off his bike, that's what he asked for.

I loved everything about that moment. It was such a sweet, innocent, and purehearted prayer coming from my small boy who struggled to speak. He was so genuine, so real, and so trusting that God would hear him. It is a precious thing when tiny children pray. They bow their heads, close their eyes, and say their prayers. Something about seeing them call on God with their childlike faith seems so right and natural; it feels reminiscent of Eden, when mankind was in perfect communion with God.

But looking around the table at my husband, parents, and three daughters, I knew that stage wouldn't last forever. Most of us have success in teaching toddlers to pray. Like my son, they seem to pick it up just by watching us and need little to no instruction. But what about when they're a little older? What happens when life gets more complicated and they grow and change into more complex individuals? What then?

I've seen a pattern in how many Christian parents, including my husband and me, approach praying with our children. For some reason, we have no problem teaching our little ones how to pray. We know exactly what to do. We tell them, "Don't eat yet; we have to pray." Then we have them close their big eyes, fold their chubby hands, and bow their heads to pray before eating. However, it seems that as soon as they grow out of that stage, we have little to offer in the way of teaching prayer. While they grow and mature, our method stays the same. We continue with the same approach from their toddlerhood: model prayer at dinner and maybe pray with them at bedtime. Our illogical hope is that their prayer life will mature even though we've continued implementing infant techniques.

A partial explanation for this may be that a part of us wants to preserve the childlike faith so often displayed in those toddler prayers. We subconsciously hope they will never outgrow praying like that. I didn't want that moment my son prayed at the dinner table to end. I wanted him to trust God like that forever. I wanted him to turn to God every time he had needs. I wanted him to never become self-conscious about prayer but to pray loudly for all to hear. I wanted him to always pray with an earnest and genuine heart. If your child is in the toddler stage now, you know exactly what I mean. However, just as refusing to buy our children larger clothes won't keep them from growing, neglecting to adjust our approach to prayer will not preserve the simple faith of their childhood.

Even if we could somehow preserve their heart in prayer, likely, none of us hopes they will still be repeating Dad at the dinner table when they're fifteen. By fifteen, they're capable of having a rich and robust relationship with God through prayer. As Christian parents, our desire is not just for our toddlers to pray but for our children of all ages to pray. And not just dinner prayers. We want our children to develop a real heart-level relationship with God that begins the moment they learn to communicate and lasts the entirety of their lives. Fortunately, there's plenty we can do to assist them in prayer throughout their childhood.

Teaching kids to pray? That's easy, right? I mean, my son picked it up with hardly any instruction. Surely, it will continue to be straightforward, won't it? Well, not exactly. When we set out to teach our children to pray, there are three main obstacles we will inevitably encounter.

Problem 1: Seeing Our Child's Nature as a Hindrance Rather Than an Advantage

"Okay, boys. Settle down. Let's close our eyes and pray." I held my son's wiggling body on my lap. Together we sat on his toddler bed while my older son, now seven, sat on the floor nearby. Both boys were outwardly ready for bed. Their teeth were clean, the potty had been used, and their bodies were wrapped in dinosaur print. Inwardly, however, they were far from ready.

I closed my eyes, hoping that as I prayed, they might settle. "God, would You give us—" I felt my toddler jerk. Tightening my arms around him slightly, I continued, "A good night's sleep. And help us to—" Another jerk. I just ignored it. "Love You and love each other." At the third jerk, I opened my eyes to see my two boys exchanging glares while they kicked each other.

Now would be a good time to admit something: I don't know how genuine my prayers were at that moment. In fact, I'm not sure I expected my boys to even listen to the words I was speaking. I think I hoped that at the very least, they might close their eyes and feel a tiny bit tired as I spoke. In other words, my sacred communing with God was just a ploy to get my boys to settle down for bed faster. It was at that moment that I thought, *Erica, you should write a book about prayer.*

I wasn't surprised they were ignoring me. I had put forth minimal effort to pray with them, but it still felt like a fail. More than a fail, actually. I felt defeated. I couldn't even get them to settle down for fake prayers, let alone real ones! I felt defeated because this wasn't an isolated event; it was just one in a long line of similar incidents. This time it was the boys kicking each other. Another time someone refused to pray. Yesterday they never even sat at all, and the time before that I got so frustrated just trying to gather everyone that when they finally came, *I* was too upset to pray.

The first problem you'll encounter, if you haven't already, is that children aren't super easy to pray with. They have a shorter attention span, a limited perspective, and a simple understanding of God and life. Though it's tempting to think praying with them will be easier when they're older, if we wait too long, we'll miss the many benefits of teaching them as young children. Despite its challenges, their childlike nature can also be a huge advantage. Consider some benefits of teaching prayer to small children:

- **Empathy.** Children, by nature, have a much easier time being empathetic. This is a huge asset when teaching children to pray for others.
- **Energy.** While we often think of their energy as being a hindrance (i.e., *They won't sit still!*), we sometimes forget that energy in prayer is a good thing. I wish more adults prayed with energy and enthusiasm. If their energy is properly directed, children can pray with great passion. And who says we need to sit still to pray anyway?
- **Faith.** As adults, our childlike faith has possibly become calloused from the hardships and disappointments of life. Our hearts struggle to pray with the same faith we had as children. Young children especially have a relatively easy time believing God to be all He says He is.
- **Honesty.** My son was not ashamed of asking God about his biking skills. Children see their desires and wrongdoings very clearly. This is huge. When we teach them about prayer early on, they develop the practice of approaching God with humility and honesty.

- **Comfort.** When we introduce prayer when they're young, children will see it as a normal part of life, unlike later, when insecurities and self-conscious thoughts can lead them to feel embarrassed or awkward in prayer, especially around others.

There are plenty of other benefits too. I have no doubt that as you journey along in teaching your children to pray, you will begin to see many more ways in which children are well positioned to engage with God. When you encounter a struggle, I encourage you to ask yourself, *How can this characteristic be turned around and used positively?*

Now is a good time to pause and pray:

> Father, let me see my child the way You do. Open my eyes to see what is beautiful and special about them now. Show me how they are uniquely positioned to seek You just as they are.

Problem 2: Thinking Maybe They'll Get It Better When They're Older

It seems like every time I hit some kind of obstacle or roadblock when it comes to teaching prayer, I can't help but sigh and think, *Maybe they'll get it when they're older.*

They don't have the attention span ... They don't understand ... I don't know any other way to explain this ... Maybe they'll get it when they're older.

There are tons of things our children won't get until they're older, but they likely won't get it even *when* they're older if we don't teach them now. Praying with our children when they're young will inform their growth and guide them as they mature. When we pray with them now, we're laying the foundation on which they will grow and mature. Just as we don't wait until our children understand true thankfulness before we instruct them to say "thank you," we shouldn't wait until they understand the complexities of prayer before we begin teaching them to pray.

 God is not waiting for our children to "grow up." ... He is engaging our children *now*.

Somewhere in the back of our adult minds we all have this little subconscious thought that "real" life doesn't begin until adulthood. We think "real" life begins when our kids begin making hard choices, when they're out there on their own in the "real" world. We tell ourselves things like, *Maybe they'll get it when they're older, it'll work out in the end, they'll eventually figure it out*, or *they'll turn out fine*, with the distant thought that what happens *when they're adults* is what's important.

There's definitely another layer of maturity that comes with adulthood, but we should reject the notion that the experiences our kids have while they're young are somehow less valuable, less formative, and in some way detached from their future adult lives. The things our children experience and learn today shape their future. But those experiences are valuable not only because they are shaping our children for tomorrow but also because they are shaping who our children are today.

And today matters.

How do we know it matters? Because God uses children!

- Moses as a baby was spared by God in the midst of a genocide.
- Miriam's courage and sense when she was just a young girl ensured her brother's safety.
- Samuel heard the audible voice of God and entered into prophetic ministry as a boy.
- David was anointed to be king of Judah when he was a young shepherd boy.
- Jeremiah was called to be a prophet to the nations before he was even a speck in the womb.
- John the Baptist was appointed to prepare the way for the Messiah before conception. Then *in his mother's womb*, he recognized the Messiah's presence.
- Mary was just a young teen when an angel appeared to give her the news that she of all women would soon carry and give birth to the Messiah.
- When Jesus was just a baby, it was revealed to Mary, Elizabeth, Joseph, the shepherds, the wise men, Anna, Simeon, and others that He was the Messiah.

God is not waiting for our children to "grow up." He's not concerned with whether they have a job yet, if they can drive, if they're still in elementary school, or if they can write their name, hold a pencil, or even walk. He is engaging our children *now*. He is pursuing them now. He has work for them to do now! And He is appointing some of them as leaders, prophets, ministers, healers, worship leaders, and preachers—now.

If we wait until our children are older to bring them to Jesus, they will miss all the opportunities to turn to Him now—when their friend betrays them, when they wrestle with telling the truth, when their parent leaves, when their grandfather dies, when their sister goes to the hospital, when they fall and break a bone, when they are sad, scared, confused, or lonely. Our children can experience God's power and comfort right now and begin to trust Him.

And it's not just sweet or cute; it's real and it's powerful.

Guess who else got the memo that children are valuable now: the Enemy. He's not waiting for them to become adults either. First Peter 5:8 says he is "prowling around like a roaring lion, looking for anyone he can devour." We see children in the Bible taken by demons, afflicted by mental illnesses, seizures, self-harm, disease, illness, and death. Today is no different; we still see all those things and more in children. More than a quarter of trafficking victims are children,[1] and school shootings have become familiar,[2] not to mention the number of children who are lost to abortion. Yep. Satan's got his finger on the pulse of the importance of children.

If we wait until our children are older to bring them to Jesus, they will miss all the opportunities to turn to Him now.

When the disciples tried to hold the children back because they were too young, too immature, too rowdy, and too messy, Jesus said, "Let the little children come to me, and do not hinder them, for the kingdom of heaven belongs to such as these" (Matt. 19:14 NIV).

If Jesus is welcoming children into His kingdom, then we'd better stop waiting till they're older and start bringing our kids to Jesus now!

Before we go any further, let's pause and pray:

> Father, show me my child's place in Your kingdom. Transform my understanding that I might see them the way You see them. Give me grace to bring them to You regularly.

Problem 3: Feeling Embarrassed about Prayer

I'm going to make a speculation: you don't feel great about your prayer life.

You think that you don't pray enough. Or that you don't pray with your kids enough. Your prayers feel dry and dull. You think you're not doing what you "should" be doing when it comes to prayer. Am I right?

If you're anything like me, you're lucky if you have a tiny bit of time to yourself before you get out of bed, and that's rarely a good time for prayer anyway. Sometimes you get sucked into your email before you even lift your head off the pillow. When you do pray on your own, it's typically on your way to work or in the middle of feeling overwhelmed, so you simply pray, *Jesus, help me.*

Family prayer is rarely better. One child doesn't like to pray. Another child uses prayer time to tell his siblings how they need to behave. *Help him to not throw his toys.* By the end of the day, you're so anxious to finally sit on the couch and watch Netflix with your spouse that bedtime prayers, if they exist, are rushed and, honestly, pathetic.

The third problem we'll face when teaching our children to pray is our own deficiencies. Guess what: you're not alone. In all my years as a Christian, I've never met a fellow Christ follower who's said, "Yeah, I'm all set with prayer. That's one area I've really nailed down." Everyone I've talked to says the opposite. They know there's *lots* of room for improvement.

So how *do* we teach our children about prayer, lead them in prayer, and answer all their questions about prayer when we feel so unqualified to do so?

Too often we invalidate ourselves from teaching something because we're not experts. According to Oxford Languages, an expert "has *comprehensive and authoritative knowledge* of a skill in a particular area"[3] (emphasis mine). When it comes to cars and medicine, I want an expert, but can anyone other than Christ say they have *comprehensive and authoritative knowledge* when it comes to talking with God?

In season seven of the TV series *Alone*, one of the contestants, Kielyn Marrone, talks about her view on being called an expert. Sitting in her dimly lit and smoky hut, she says, "At the beginning of each show … it says, 'Warning, these are trained survival experts … do not attempt this at home….' I'm never gonna call myself an expert…. I mean, an expert in anything limits yourself from continuing to learn. But what I can say is that this is athletics, mental athletics."[4]

Though Kielyn was considered an expert by History Channel standards, she considered it a negative label. She realized that calling herself an expert meant that she had already learned everything there was to learn. I love that she was humble enough to see this. We will never learn all there is to learn or "arrive" when it comes to prayer. Far be it from us to ever think we have authoritative knowledge when it comes to speaking with our Lord.

So, rather than feel guilty about prayer or wish we were some kind of expert, let's embrace the idea that we are *not* experts in this field and humbly accept that we have ample room to grow. If you've been sitting there feeling crummy about your prayer life because you've not measured up to some standard, consider this your invitation to reject any shame or guilt associated with prayer and any expectation that you should be some perfect example who prays every moment. Instead, let's start fresh like a student on the first day of school with a new box of crayons. The reality is, we all have plenty of room to learn and grow.

Before moving on, take a moment to genuinely pray the following:

> Father, my heart's desire is to seek You more and teach my children to do the same. I'm letting go of any guilt or shame I feel about prayer and positioning myself to learn. Moving forward, I'm leaning on Your grace to help me.

Chapter 3

I'M NO EXPERT ...
BUT I CAN BE
A GUIDE

"Rub a few of these together, and tell me what you smell." We were only twenty minutes from my home, at a park we'd visited dozens of times, but I was learning things I never knew. I grabbed the end of a twig, stripped the needles off into my hand, and began rolling them between my fingertips. Bringing them up to my nose, I took a deep whiff. "It smells like Christmas!" I perked up. "Well, yes, it smells piney," the guide said with a chuckle, "but it has a citrus scent as well. The pine trees that have a citrus smell are eastern hemlocks."

Not only had I never thought of rubbing pine needles between my fingers in order to smell them better, but it also hadn't occurred to me that one could identify pine trees based on scent. To me, they were all just different variations of "Christmassy."

As we hiked along, I learned about rock formations, seasonal patterns, the history of the land, and more. It was my first guided hike. I'd never bothered to do a guided hike before because I knew how to follow trails and that's all a guide helps with, right? Well, no. They help you discover and learn along the trail. What might have been a grueling hike up the mountain turned out to be a delight with a guide teaching us and pointing things out along the way.

Remember how my relationship with Christ began? I was alone in my bedroom, just reading my little Bible. No one forced me to sit there and read. Had my mom sent me to my room and commanded me to read my Bible, I doubt I would've walked out saved!

We are not going to teach our children, model prayer, and lead them in prayer as professionals. We won't dictate their duties as taskmasters and then sit back passively and hope they get it. Instead, we will position ourselves as guides. We'll travel with them, teach as we go, and gradually move alongside them so they mature.

Our role is simple: be *guides* who bring our children to Jesus and lay a foundation for prayer.

The Way We Teach

I never enjoyed history or found it interesting until tenth grade. I can't tell you any specific facts I learned from class that year and, sadly, I can't even remember my teacher's name. But I can tell you that in that class I discovered history was interesting, fascinating, exciting, and sometimes funny. Realizing this had nothing to do with our textbooks or what time period we learned about. I discovered a love for history because of the *way* my teacher taught. He bounced around the room telling story after story. To him, history was not fact after fact to be absorbed but story after story to be told. He was engaging and goofy. Because of the way he taught, I discovered the delight of history.

The *way* we teach our children matters. The *way* we lead them matters. They may not remember the details of what we prayed, but they will remember our attitude toward prayer. In fact, the way we pray and talk about prayer will determine the impression they have of prayer for years. What impression do we want to give our children about prayer? How do we want them to view prayer?

Just as there were qualities about my teacher that made him a great teacher, there are certain qualities that can make us great guides. Let's look at those now.

 The way we pray and talk about prayer will determine the impression they have of prayer for years.

A Good Guide Is Accessible

Have you seen advertisements for MasterClass? It's a membership program where for a monthly fee you gain access to loads of classes taught by people who are "masters" in their fields, everything from cooking to psychology. If you saw those ads, you likely considered becoming a member during the summer of 2020. I know I did.

Those classes are probably great and full of information, but as much as online teachers try to teach in an accessible way, they are not actually accessible. They are on one side of the screen while we are on the other. We are separate and do not have access to them.

When we went on that guided hike, I could have asked our guide any questions I wanted to. He was right there with us. This man may have been an expert in his field, but he wasn't acting like one. He was acting as our guide. While a professional may sit back and teach from a leather chair, a guide walks alongside you and endures the same terrain and travels the same trail.

Jesus was an excellent model in accessibility for us. John 1:14a says, "The Word became flesh and *dwelt among us*." Jesus left His throne in heaven to be with us, walk with us, eat with us, and suffer as we suffer.

As we consider our role as prayer guides for our children, let's be sure our children see us as accessible and approachable. We are not set apart from them, pointing out what they should do; instead, we travel with them, at their pace, and try to see what they see. This may look like taking time to listen to their concerns, praying at "inconvenient" times, and praying about things that are important to them even if they aren't to us.

A Good Guide Is Discerning

During our guided hike, not everyone in our group was able to walk up the mountain at the same pace. While the children were trying to run ahead, a couple of ladies lagged behind. Rather than plow on and make the hike miserable for the ladies in the back, our guide had us all pause often for water breaks. Not only that, but he also regularly went to the back of the group to check in with and encourage the stragglers. I'm so thankful he noticed the difficulty they were having. If he hadn't, they would've eventually either turned back or given up trying to hike with the group.

As we teach our children to pray and raise them to have a genuine relationship with God, the last thing we want to do is turn prayer into a burden. I praise God that prayer was not imposed on me as a religious task. Prayer has primarily been a beautiful and intimate thing for me.

For this reason, I take a cautious approach to prayer in my own home because I don't want prayer to be seen as a duty. You may have felt similarly. Maybe you've thought something along the lines of *Wouldn't it be better if we let them pick up prayer on their own? If we're too pushy, they won't want to pray at all.* In our worry about doing it wrong, it's easy to conclude that perhaps inaction might be better than action.

We don't want to push too hard and lose them, but we also don't want to wait at the bottom of the mountain and hope they'll make it up to the top on their own. The solution? Lead *with discernment.* We still need to lead, but we can be discerning in the *way* we lead.

As discerning guides, we'll pay close attention to those we are leading. We'll be thoughtful and considerate as we evaluate their needs. We'll lead with confidence but also tenderness. Are they tired and in need of a break, or are they ready for a challenge? Our goal as discerning guides is for them to get further *with us* than they would on their own.

A Good Guide Is a Model

A friend of mine and her three children were walking through a very hard season. As she was telling her kids about God's faithfulness one morning, one child pushed back. "How do you know He's faithful? Maybe He's not!" Quick to her defense, her other child jumped in: "How dare you say that? You know Mom prays every morning in that chair. She would know if God is faithful."

In that difficult season, my friend had been needing God more than ever, and though she had little capacity to do much else, she prayed. And her children saw it. She didn't just pray out loud at the dinner table or tell her kids to say their prayers before bed, though I'm sure she did that too. She modeled something much more. She modeled that she was dependent on God for her needs. She showed her children that she drew strength from Him, leaned on Him, and turned to Him every day. She demonstrated that prayer was how she stayed tethered to God amid a storm.

Our children will learn more by seeing us pray than by being taught all the "right things" about prayer. No, we're not always going to be perfect models or get everything right. But we can still be good models. We can let them see us pray, we can let them hear us pray, and we can tell them how God encourages us when we pray. We can model how to lean on God, trust Him, depend on Him, and turn to Him in all we do.

We've taken a thorough look at what makes a good guide. Our next step as guides is to discover how to lay a foundation for prayer in our children's lives. We do this by bringing the practice and habit of prayer into our homes and weaving prayer into the fabric of our everyday lives.

Lay a Foundation for Prayer in the Home

Raise your hand if you'd like something to add to your to-do list. Yeah, me neither.

Unfortunately, prayer can sometimes feel like another thing to do. And given how busy most parents are, it can be hard to see how or when meaningful prayer is ever going to happen. If you already feel overwhelmed or stressed out, listen closely: prayer doesn't need to be another "task" during the day; you can simply integrate prayer into the day you already have. Don't believe me? Let's have a look at Deuteronomy 6:6–7:

> These words that I am giving you today are to be in your heart. Repeat them to your children. Talk about them when you sit in your house and when you walk along the road, when you lie down and when you get up.

I don't believe this passage is meant to be taken literally, in that those are the exact and only times we should talk about God. The examples listed—sitting at home, walking along the road, lying down, and getting up—can be grouped into two categories: planned and unplanned activities. Planned activities are when we lie down and when we get up. If nothing else, you can guarantee these events will happen each day. The second group of events are more spontaneous in nature—when we're walking along or sitting around.

Some parents approach prayer with a checklist mentality. *We pray before leaving for school in the morning, we pray before eating, and we pray before bedtime.* They do a great job making prayer a practice and a habit but not much else. On the other hand, some approach prayer as something to do in dire times. *Dad lost his job; let's pray,* or, *Your brother's sick; we need to pray.* This is valuable too. Children need to see us turning to God in times of need, though those shouldn't be the only times.

The picture we get from this passage is that both the regular, habitual practice of prayer *and* the spontaneous times of prayer are needed. Let's unpack this idea more. I believe that understanding this concept is key to seeing the beauty of prayer and not mistaking it as a burden or another task to complete.

Planned Prayer

The hike I mentioned earlier was the first of several guided hikes, one of which took place in the Appalachian Mountains of Virginia. The guide brought a small boom box along with him. I wasn't sure why until the path led us to a small clearing in the woods. At that time, our guide signaled for us to be still and quiet; then he set the player on a stump and pushed Play.

We all listened while it played the call of a certain type of owl. This owl causes small birds to act territorial. Thinking an owl was invading their space, one after another, small nuthatches made their way over to the clearing and started climbing down nearby trees toward the boom box. It was fascinating. We didn't go out of the way for this activity; it happened along the trail, but the guide knew this clearing was on the trail, so he planned to have us all stop for a teaching opportunity.

When we look at prayer as another thing to do, we end up viewing our busy schedules and thinking to ourselves, *The day is so busy. Where will prayer fit in?* I hear you! However, there are activities we are *already* doing that would be opportune times to pray together. Think of these activities like the clearing in the woods; the guide knew we would reach it, and he planned that we would pause when we did. Rather than ask yourself, "Where do I have extra time?" ask yourself, "What activities are we already doing that would be opportune times to pray?"

Though I doubt we've ever said it out loud, there are two times a day my husband and I *plan* to pray with our children. Those two times are hitched to activities that happen every day without fail: dinner and bedtime. We know, even on the worst days, dinner will happen. Even if it's cereal, we will eat dinner. Even if Daddy is working late or someone's still at practice, whoever's home will sit and eat something. So we plan to pray during that activity because we know, just like the clearing on the trail, it's coming.

Bedtime is similar. I've yet to live a day with no bedtime; at some point in every day the kids will go to bed. It doesn't always look the same. Sometimes the older ones stay up late doing homework, but every day without fail my children go to bed. Because that activity is bound to happen, we plan to make prayer a part of their bedtime routine.

 As we brave the role of teaching our children about prayer, we can think of ourselves as guides who simply point things out along the way.

Does this mean we always pray at dinner? No. Honestly, sometimes I forget. Does this mean we always pray at bedtime?

No. But I don't always brush my kids' teeth either! The point is that our dinner and bedtime routines include prayer, so we usually pray at those times.

What does your day look like? What activities make up your day, and where can you weave prayer into them? Where can you *plan* to pray?

Maybe you drive your two children to school in the morning. It's already a part of your day to spend time in the car with those two kids. That may be a great time to plan on praying. Each day you likely put your kids to bed. Maybe you brush their teeth and read a bedtime story. That activity would be a perfect place to incorporate some prayer time.

One of the greatest benefits of planned prayer is that our children see that prayer is a priority. It's not just something we do when we feel like it or when it's convenient. We make prayer a priority because it's valuable. When we model prayer as a priority, we begin to lay the foundation for prayer that we've talked about.

Unplanned Prayer

I was never a very good student in school. It wasn't that I didn't have good teachers or that I wasn't smart. The problem was the format: sitting down to memorize facts and information I never asked to learn in the first place. It was all too forced.

The best part about learning from the guide on our hike was that all the learning happened so naturally. The guide pointed out interesting features of the land *as* we hiked. It wasn't a school-style lecture; rather, learning was woven into it.

As we brave the role of teaching our children about prayer, we can think of ourselves as guides who simply point things out along the way. In the journey of life, we simply remind, teach, and point our children to Jesus. Whether we're on our way to school or eating breakfast together, we have countless opportunities to incorporate prayer into our daily lives and engage our children in the process.

When we plan to pray, we tie prayer into activities that are already happening each day. Unplanned prayer, however, is not so much about the activities we are doing as much as it is about *noticing* opportunities throughout the day to pray. I doubt the guide on the first hike I described planned to point out the scent of the eastern hemlock, but as we came upon it, he decided to. With unplanned or spontaneous praying, we let cues from the day spark our prayers.

Although they don't have to be, good cues are often our daily struggles: your son getting a rug burn on the trampoline, your daughter feeling anxious about a conflict with her friend, a sick family member, your child feeling nervous about a test. Instead of feeling burdened or overwhelmed by problems, look at them as cues to pray. As you do, you'll be showing your children who you ultimately trust in. Isaiah 31:1 says:

> Woe to those who go down to Egypt for help
> and rely on horses,
> who trust in chariots because they are many
> and in horsemen because they are very strong,

> but do not look to the Holy One of Israel
> or consult the LORD! (ESV)

In times of trouble, there are a myriad of things we can turn to for help or comfort. Sure, things like a YouTube tutorial may help us change a flat tire, but where we ultimately put our hope is of great importance. When we shepherd our children in prayer—specifically, spontaneous prayer—we are helping them cultivate a heart that turns to God first and above all else.

As we practice this, we're going to get really good at picking up on cues and recognizing opportunities to pray along the way. We'll find ourselves praying for friends, leaders, teachers, governments, and schools. We'll find ourselves asking God for healing, guidance, breakthrough, comfort, discernment, wisdom, and much more!

 With unplanned or spontaneous prayer, we let cues from the day spark our prayers.

A Different Route

After a year in our new home, I finally found the fastest way to church. Knowing the fastest route helped, but it didn't make up for everyone running late. One Sunday, after we were finally in the car, I discovered there was a giant blockade at the end of our road. An entire path was blocked off for a race that was happening through our city that morning. *Are you kidding me? Who has a race on Sunday anyway?* Turns out, lots of people.

I turned around and went a different way; that was blocked off too. So I made a right turn, hoping that way was open. Nope, blockade there too. Finally, after a dozen or so turns, I found my way out of all the blockades and was en route to church. As I drove down the road, there were people on either side with flags and water jugs. *What is everyone doing here?* Turns out I had managed to get my minivan onto the race road! Bystanders were out there waving and ready to pass out water, when along came a mom driving a van full of kids. Whoops! We all laughed as I drove on and waved happily to the spectators.

Sometimes the route that seems best won't work. That doesn't mean our destination is off; we may just need to find another way to get there. When we're determined to disciple our children and point them to Jesus in prayer, we'll find what works. We may just have to weave around a bit until we find the best way to get there. And like my experience that Sunday, the path we end up taking may be a tad unconventional.

Some of the examples I share throughout this book are not going to work for your children or your family situation. That's okay. There is not a perfect, correct, or ideal way to pray with our children. You might be able to tell immediately that some methods are not right for your situation, or you may have to try them first.

A friend of mine has both adopted and birth children with ADHD and various degrees of autism. When talking about family prayer time with her five kids, she said, "I had to give up on the idea that we could all pray together as a family or have devotions after dinner. We tried for a long time until I finally realized it didn't work for us." It wasn't until later that she realized what *would* work for them. Their path to prayer wasn't the most obvious one, but they found other ways. She and her husband still pray with and disciple their children, but it looks much different from what many families do. (More on their solution in chapter 9.)

If your child is very young, first, I want to commend you for wanting to establish prayer in the lives of your children no matter how little they are. This is *huge*. Bravo! Second, when you come across an idea that seems too old for your child, be encouraged. By being aware of it now, you'll be able to adjust your methods *as* they grow and mature.

> **Pro Tip:** Stick some Post-it notes on pages you want to come back to when your children are a little older!

Keep It Simple

One morning, my oldest daughter, who was quite young at the time, walked into the kitchen after having barely climbed out of bed. We chatted a little, and then I asked her, "Do you remember any of your dreams?" "Yes," she responded. So I said, "Oh, what did you dream about?" She replied, "Jesus." I stopped what I was doing. *Jesus was in her dreams? Did she receive a word from God?*

Trying not to appear too excited, I put extra effort into keeping my tone calm. "What was He doing in your dreams?" Without hesitation, she simply replied, "He was playing with my toys." (Insert melting-heart emoji.) Here I was preparing myself for something profound, and while it was certainly profound, what made it profound was its simplicity.

We have a tendency to complicate things and think they are more difficult than they actually are. But, beloved, don't miss this: Jesus communicated His love for my daughter by playing with her toys. How simple. How easy. Sometimes the most profound things happen in the simplest ways.

The next chapter is going to look at the theology of prayer. And following that we'll discuss ideas to engage our children in prayer, praying one on one with our children, and more. But in all that you're going to learn, remember to keep it simple. Prayer is simple. So simple a three-year-old can pick it up.

We needn't force anything, push for certain outcomes, or put pressure on seeing fruit from it. Though our instruction should grow as our children are able to comprehend more, we should never move away from the heart of prayer: prayer is how our hearts connect with God's.

> Father God, help me to be a great guide. Help me to lead gently and with discernment. God, show me where we can plan to pray together as a family, but also open my eyes to see the myriad opportunities to seek You with my children throughout the course of each day.

Chapter 4

THE THEOLOGY OF PRAYER

I was in the kitchen one morning when Malachi came down the steps. He sat down on the last stair so our new puppy could jump onto his lap to say good morning. Noticing he was wearing different clothes—though not necessarily clean ones—I commended him. "Wow, son, you're all dressed!" Being the youngest, combined with being homeschooled, he typically wears the same clothes every day.

His response surprised me. "I got dressed because I'm going to Grandma Sue's house today for four sleepovers." A little confused, I inquired, "Oh, why do you think that?" Without hesitating, he replied, "Because I prayed at the table last night that I would have four sleepovers."

It was true. He had been in rare form the night before and volunteered to pray at dinner. He'd said little, but in his prayer, he asked God for four sleepovers at Grandma's house. I paused for a moment, pondering his presumed logic. God hears our prayers and as our good Father, He loves to give good gifts to His children.

Clearly, Malachi lacked no faith when he prayed. Why shouldn't he now expect to have those sleepovers?

This question is a valid one. We don't want to teach our children that some prayers aren't important to God. On the other hand, we don't want our children to treat prayer as if God were a genie, here to grant our wishes. This quandary and a myriad of others will inevitably come up regarding prayer.

What happens when we pray? Why do bad things happen even when we pray? What is prayer? This chapter is going to take a look at the theology of prayer. Don't be scared by the word *theology*. It simply means the truth about prayer according to the Bible.

If I were you, I'd be incredibly tempted to skip this chapter about brainy facts and jump into the practical steps and how-tos. In fact, I even considered moving this chapter toward the end of the book for that exact reason. But here's the thing: the value of prayer can't take root in our children's hearts if they don't have a biblical *understanding* of prayer.

Questions will arise, and your "Malachi" will need guidance. Learning the theology of prayer will provide you with a foundational, biblical understanding, so when your four-year-old wonders why her fish died even though she prayed, you can give her a solid answer. Additionally, this chapter will walk through simple language for complex ideas.

> **Pro Tip:** My hope is you'll regularly return to this chapter as a resource to help explain the foundations of prayer as questions arise.

The value of prayer can't take root in our children's hearts if they don't have a biblical *understanding* of prayer.

Back to my son on the steps. What answer do we give Malachi as he sits all dressed and ready to go? Well, there is not one "right" answer as much as there are several truths about prayer and multiple conversations that need to be had. For instance, Malachi clearly knew that God heard his prayer for sleepovers and that God is powerful enough to make anything happen. I feel proud that he knew these simple truths. However, there were some other truths he was now ready to learn as well. And this situation was a perfect opportunity to teach him those.

My husband often talks about "living in the tension." I've heard this phrase so many times, I'm tempted to roll my eyes when he says it. But the statement is valid and especially important when it comes to prayer. Saying we "live in the tension" regarding prayer means we are living in the intersection of multiple things being true and equally important. Oftentimes trouble comes when we are well versed in some truths but not others, or when we elevate some truths over others.

I love creative playground structures, especially ones that can handle adult play. One such structure I've seen built in a few different shapes is a net-like construction with ropes running every which way. The ropes are all in equal tension, and because they are woven together, they are also equally valid in how they support each other. Because of this, even an adult can enjoy the whole structure and play all over it.

Our culture tends toward extremes in everything from fashion to theology, but when we give equal value to all the truths about God and prayer, like the netted structure with equally supporting ropes, we will have a robust and healthy prayer life. If however, we overemphasize some truths and underemphasize others, we set both ourselves and our children up for a shaky and confusing faith.

Recently my oldest son, now seven, shared with me that he'd prayed for a pet eagle when he was younger. Wanting one so badly, he even asked his sister to take on his request in prayer. With sympathy for his young faith, I gave him a hug and said, "I'm sorry, buddy." When I asked him why he thought God sometimes doesn't give us everything we ask for, he didn't hesitate: "Because we don't always need it."

The truth is that God gives us what we need, and we can trust Him to determine *what* that is and *when* that is. My son's faith was not shaken by this experience. He knew God had heard his prayers and that He cares for us. Now he also knows God gives us what we need. This truth does not lessen the other truth or shake our faith. If anything, it makes it more secure. In fact, the more our children understand the truths about prayer, the more they will walk in the power of prayer.

There is no need to get nervous or flustered when our children have questions or seem frustrated or even confused. This is because, while we have a role as parents, so does God, and therefore we can entrust our children—doubts and all—to Him. When our children have questions, they are likely ready to learn a new truth. We'll teach these truths gradually and at a pace that suits their age and understanding. All these truths will work together to form a net on which our children can climb, enjoying much prayer, faith, and trust in Jesus.

 The more our children understand the truths about prayer, the more they will walk in the power of prayer.

While entire books have been written on the theology of prayer, this chapter attempts to break down that theology into simple truth statements. These statements and their explanations are broken into three age groups based on my own experience in ministry: three-to-five-year-olds, six-to-eight-year-olds, and children nine years old and older. These ranges are meant to be used as a guide; the majority of children in each age group will be able to understand the concepts. Many of the concepts build upon each other, so teaching them in order will be helpful.

Theology can be intimidating, so I've worded much of the following sections as if I were speaking directly to children in that age group. While you don't need to read to your children from this book (though you can if you'd like), the intent is to give you language you can use to communicate big ideas. Some truths have a "Taking It Further" section. Once your child has a solid understanding of the basic concept, bring them back to that truth again when they're older, but take them a little further.

Here are some theological truths to teach your children.

For Three-to-Five-Year-Olds
1. Prayer is talking with God.

> King Hezekiah and the prophet Isaiah son of
> Amoz prayed about this and *cried out* to heaven.
> (2 Chron. 32:20)

When we talk to God, we call it "praying." When we pray, our hearts speak to God's heart. We can talk to God out loud or just in our hearts. We can talk with God about all kinds of things. If you had a great day, you can thank Him for it. If you're feeling sad, you can tell Him that too.

Sometimes it's easier to talk with God when we are alone because we're not distracted by other things, but God can hear us no matter what we're doing, where we are, or what time it is. While we may pray more by ourselves, God also likes it when we pray with others.

Taking It Further

Asking God for things for ourselves or others is an important part of prayer, but there are actually many kinds of prayer. When we worship and praise or thank God, that's prayer. When we confess (or tell) our sins to Him and ask Him to forgive us, that's also prayer. Anytime we talk to God about anything, we are praying.

2. God loves when we talk with Him.

> The eyes of the Lord are on the righteous
> and his ears are open to their prayer. (1 Pet. 3:12a)

> May my prayer be set before you as incense,
> the raising of my hands as the evening offering
> (Ps. 141:2)

> Each one had a harp and golden bowls filled
> with incense, which are the prayers of the saints.
> (Rev. 5:8b)

God loves to hear the voices of His children. He is never too busy or too distracted, and He always wants to hear what we have to say. The Bible describes our prayers as a wonderful scent that rises up to God. When we pray, we can imagine that, just like a beautiful-smelling candle, our prayers smell so nice to God.

Taking It Further

When God first created people in the garden of Eden, He walked right next to them. They had a close relationship with Him. When Adam and Eve disobeyed God, evil and sin were invited into God's perfect world. Sin ruined the closeness we were meant to have with God and has since separated people from Him. God sent His Son,

Jesus, to fix the separation between God and His people. Jesus died on the cross to mend the broken relationship so that through faith in Him, you and I and all God's people could have a relationship with Him again. If Jesus died so we could be with God, we can be sure that He *loves* to talk with His sons and daughters!

3. All good things come from God.

> Every good and perfect gift is from above, coming
> down from the Father of lights. (James 1:17a)

Because God loves us so much, He wants to show His love for us. He even sent His Son, Jesus, to us. That's how much He loves us. When we receive a gift or have a good day, we should thank God. The Bible says that all good things are gifts from God.

4. Not everything we pray for will happen, but we can trust God no matter what.

> We know that all things work together for the good
> of those who love God, who are called according
> to his purpose. (Rom. 8:28)

> My God will supply all your needs according to his
> riches in glory in Christ Jesus. (Phil. 4:19)

> As heaven is higher than earth,
> so my ways are higher than your ways,
> and my thoughts than your thoughts. (Isa. 55:9)

Not everything we ask God for will happen, but remember that God loves us tremendously. Because He loves us, we can trust that He knows what's best for us and will be with us no matter what happens. God has promised to work out all things for our good and always give us what we need.

Taking It Further

Sometimes, no matter how hard we pray and no matter how much faith we pray with, sad things will still happen. There is not an easy answer for this. Isaiah 55:9 says, "As the heavens are higher than the earth, so are my ways higher than your ways and my thoughts than your thoughts" (NIV).

Generally speaking, bad things can happen despite our prayers, for a few reasons. First, earth is full of sin, evil, and brokenness, unlike heaven. As a result, there will be pain and suffering until Jesus returns and makes things new (see Luke 21:25–28; Rev. 21:1–5).

Second, sometimes God allows hard things to happen because He has a bigger plan and purpose. For example, Jesus dying a painful death was part of God's good plan, but the disciples didn't think so. They didn't want that to happen. Thankfully, Jesus not only knew God had a plan, but He also chose to follow it.

Last, sometimes bad things happen as a result of our own sin and poor choices. For instance, if we eat ice cream for breakfast, lunch, and dinner, we'll likely get sick and feel terrible. The good news is that even when we sin or make bad choices, God is still in control and loves us.

For Six-to-Eight-Year-Olds
5. God wants us to pray for others too.

> First of all, then, I urge that petitions, prayers, intercessions, and thanksgivings be made for everyone. (1 Tim. 2:1)

We can pray for others and ask God to help them. When we or other people are sick, hurting, or in need, we should pray for them and ask God to help. The Bible is full of wonderful stories of people being saved, rescued, healed, and brought back to life because of others' prayers for them. (More on praying for others in chapter 6.)

6. Prayer is important for our relationship with God.

> Draw near to God, and he will draw near to you. (James 4:8a)

> I am the vine; you are the branches. The one who remains in me and I in him produces much fruit, because you can do nothing without me. (John 15:5)

Remaining in Jesus means we obey Him, trust Him, and try to know Him more. One way we do this is by spending time talking to Him. Just as we can't have a good relationship with someone we've never talked to, we can't have a good relationship with God if we never talk with Him. We want to have as close of a relationship with God as possible, so we should talk with Him often.

Taking It Further

Jesus offers us "living water" (John 7:37–38). Just as we can't survive without water, our soul—our very inner self—is not healthy without Jesus. Spending time with God allows us to connect with Him, learn to recognize His voice, align our hearts with His, and know Him better.

7. God can speak to us.

> My sheep hear my voice, I know them, and they
> follow me. (John 10:27)

> When the Spirit of truth comes, he will guide you
> into all the truth. For he will not speak on his own,
> but he will speak whatever he hears. He will also
> declare to you what is to come. (John 16:13)

> Call to me and I will answer you and tell you great
> and incomprehensible things you do not know.
> (Jer. 33:3)

God can speak to us through His Holy Spirit. He can speak to our hearts or minds. When the Holy Spirit speaks to us, He sometimes speaks to us in words, a Bible verse, or even just a feeling that encourages us. God can also speak to us through people or events. Occasionally, God may even speak in such a way that we hear Him with our ears. Though this is rare, stories in the Bible tell of it happening a few times. The clearest way God speaks to us is through His Word, the Bible. Because God speaks to us, it's important that when we pray, we take time to quiet our minds and let Him talk too.

Taking It Further

Because we are creative people, we can sometimes think God is speaking to us when He is not. So that we will know it's Him, God will never speak anything that doesn't agree with the Bible or His own character. It's always a good idea to ask another Christian and compare what we heard or felt with what the Bible says.

8. God wants our hearts to be honest and clean when we pray.

> LORD, you have searched me and known me.
> You know when I sit down and when I stand up;
> you understand my thoughts from far away.
> (Ps. 139:1–2)

> Let us draw near with a true heart in full assurance of faith, with our hearts sprinkled clean from an evil conscience and our bodies washed in pure water. (Heb. 10:22)

> If I had cherished iniquity in my heart,
>   the Lord would not have listened. (Ps. 66:18 ESV)

God knows all things, even our thoughts. In fact, Jesus sometimes answered questions that people only thought but never asked. If God knows even our thoughts, there's no need to hide anything from Him. Since we couldn't hide anything from God even if we wanted to, it's important to be honest when we pray.

God wants us to have a close and special relationship with Him, but we can't have one if we're not honest with Him. Part of being honest with God includes admitting, or telling the truth about, things we've done that were wrong. This is also called confession. If we refuse to admit, or confess, our sin, it's as if we are keeping God at a distance.

We can sometimes feel uncomfortable admitting the things we've done wrong, but God wants us to do this so He can forgive us. When we have faith in Jesus, He promises to forgive us for all our sins. When God forgives us, it's like He cleanses our hearts of any wrong we have done. After David confessed his sin to God, he prayed, "Cleanse me ... and I will be clean; wash me, and I will be whiter than snow" (Ps. 51:7 NIV). We can pray this too.

Taking It Further

When Jesus washed His disciples' feet, Peter objected, but Jesus told him, "Unless I wash you, you have no part with me." Peter changed his mind. "Then, Lord," he said, "not just my feet but my hands and my head as well!" Jesus' answer was interesting. He said, "Those who have had a bath need only to wash their feet; their whole body is clean" (John 13:8b–10a NIV).

In Roman culture, baths were a popular way to wash, but after people walked around the dirty and dusty streets, their feet were very dirty. The bath Jesus was talking about represents the one-time repentance that happens when we put our faith and trust in Him and receive forgiveness for the first time. This saves our souls and eternally cleanses us of our sin. But, just as we have to wash our dirty feet, we need to regularly confess and repent; this keeps our hearts in line with God's heart. When we confess our sins, we are simply admitting guilt about our wrongdoings. We repent by turning away from those sins and toward God.

Additionally, there is no sin that is too big for God to forgive. And while we sometimes get tired of asking Him to forgive us over and over, God never tires of forgiving us. As many times as we are willing to ask, God is willing to forgive.

For Children Nine Years Old and Older
9. God listens to our prayers because of Jesus.

> Your iniquities are separating you
> from your God,
> and your sins have hidden his face from you
> so that he does not listen. (Isa. 59:2)

> Whatever you ask in my name, I will do it so that the Father may be glorified in the Son. (John 14:13)

> Since we have boldness to enter the sanctuary through the blood of Jesus ... let us draw near with a true heart in full assurance of faith, with our hearts sprinkled clean from an evil conscience and our bodies washed in pure water. (Heb. 10:19, 22)

Our sin separates us from God. When Jesus died on the cross, He paid the punishment for our sin with His death so we could have a relationship with Him now and for all eternity. Through our faith in Jesus, sin no longer separates us from God. Therefore, it is only because of Jesus that God listens to us! The verses in Hebrews say we can confidently come to God because our hearts have been cleansed by the blood of Jesus. This is also why we often end our prayers by saying, "In Jesus' name." This statement declares that we have faith in Jesus and that according to God's own promise, He will hear our prayers.

Taking It Further

In the Old Testament, God chose a special place to be near the people. But the only people allowed in this special place, which was eventually called the temple, were priests. Even the priests could not just waltz into God's magnificent and holy presence without following a lot of rules, such as wearing special clothes, almost like a uniform, that were sprinkled with some blood and oil from an offering. This may sound odd to us, but the blood and oil showed that a payment was made to cover the cost, or debt, of their sin. Only in these special clothes, showing they had no sin, were the priests seen as clean and allowed to enter God's holy presence.

When we place our faith in Jesus, *His* blood "covers" all our sin, so we too can be seen as clean and perfect. When we pray, we can imagine that God welcomes us, like the priests, into His holy presence and that He sees us as clean and perfect as Jesus.

10. Our prayers have a special role in God's plan.

> The prayer of a righteous person is very powerful
> in its effect. Elijah was a human being as we are,
> and he prayed earnestly that it would not rain, and
> for three years and six months it did not rain on
> the land. (James 5:16b–17)

> "Don't be afraid, Daniel," he said to me, "for from
> the first day that you purposed to understand and
> to humble yourself before your God, your prayers
> were heard. I have come because of your prayers."
> (Dan. 10:12)

Jesus prayed to His Father, "Your kingdom come. Your will
be done on earth as it is in heaven" (Matt. 6:10). God's perfect will
happens in heaven, but it doesn't always happen here. On earth,
not everyone listens to God or obeys Him or does what is right.
There are many things about life that are not right. One thing we
can do to change this is pray. Jesus prayed for the world, but we
can start small if we'd like. We can pray, "Let Your will be done
here in my school as it is in heaven."

We are told in the book of James that the prophet Elijah was a
person like us, yet he kept it from *raining* with his prayers! Daniel
dedicated himself to prayer for three weeks. Then, while he was
standing by a river, an angel appeared to him. We are told that
because of his prayers, the angel responded and came to him.

Although our God is sovereign, which means He's in control
of all things, He uses our prayers to change things here on earth.

In fact, it's part of our job as Christians to pray for God's will. And just as Elijah's prayers stopped the rain, things can change here because of our prayers too.

11. When we don't know what to pray, the Holy Spirit prays for us.

> The Spirit also helps us in our weakness, because we do not know what to pray for as we should, but the Spirit himself intercedes for us with inexpressible groanings. (Rom. 8:26)

Sometimes our hearts hurt and we know we need God but we don't know what to pray. The book of Romans says that the Holy Spirit will pray for us when we don't know what to pray. That means when we look to God, even though we may not know what to pray and we may not be thinking in complete sentences or even words, because of the Holy Spirit, God hears our prayers.

12. We should want God's will and glory first.

> He made his glorious strength
> available at the right hand of Moses,
> divided the water before them
> to make an eternal name for *himself.* (Isa. 63:12)

> Father, if you are willing, take this cup away from me—nevertheless, not my will, but yours, be done. (Luke 22:42)

> Seek first the kingdom of God and his righteous-
> ness, and all these things will be provided for you.
> (Matt. 6:33)

In all we may want, need, or desire, we can be confident that God's will is always best. When Jesus was about to suffer, He prayed, "Father, if you are willing, take this cup [of suffering] away from me—nevertheless, not my will, but *yours*, be done" (Luke 22:42). When we pray things like "But God, let Your will be done," we don't need to be afraid of what He might do. In fact, we can be extremely confident that what He wants is always best! As we practice putting God's will ahead of our own, we'll find our desires shifting to be more like His. This is the work of the Holy Spirit in us.

Additionally, we know that God's glory is more important than anything we may want for ourselves. Thankfully, Jesus gives us clear instruction regarding our life and prayers: seek God and the things of God first, and everything else will be taken care of (see Matt. 6:33).

Last, over all these truths, don't forget to share that there is mystery in God. This is why we keep seeking, keep asking, keep studying, and keep praying. The sum of Him cannot fit in our hands, let alone our heads. We cannot possibly teach all the truths about God because we cannot comprehend all the truths about God. Bible scholars debate about verses all the time because there are some things that aren't crystal clear. The good news is, what's important is clear. When teaching truths and answering questions, don't teach the mystery out of God; there are plenty of things we don't fully understand, and that's okay.

Malachi did get those sleepovers. But it was a few days later and our schedules only allowed for a couple at a time, so they weren't consecutive. It turned out to be a perfect picture of how God responds to our prayers—not always how we think and often not with the timing we hope for. No doubt our children will have questions, and they may misunderstand some things about prayer. We can reassure them of these core truths as those questions and concerns arise. Better yet, the older they get, the more we can start pointing them to the Bible to search out answers on their own.

Chapter 5

THE BIGGEST SECRET

Preparing to Pray

Recently, after reading several articles about events that were taking place across the globe, I was disturbed. My heart ached as I pondered them and considered how to respond. Twenty minutes later, my children and I were on our knees, praying for God to intervene with power for a people group they had never heard of who lived on the other side of the world.

What happened in those twenty minutes? Are my children simply amazing? Well, yes, actually. Or am I an outstanding mother? I'd love for you to think so, though I'm pretty sure that once I explain what happened, you'll see that I'm not that clever after all.

The On-Ramp

Imagine you're shopping at Target when you see a friend heading toward you. She greets you with "Hey! How's it going?" But before you have a chance to answer, she continues with "Will you pray with me?" Then, without leaving any pause, she bows her head and starts praying.

How engaged in prayer would you be at that moment? My guess is, not very. As if replaying a car crash, your mind would likely be trying to put together the pieces of what just happened. *I was walking down the aisle. I saw my friend coming toward me ... We greeted each other. But I'm drawing a blank ... What happened next? Why are we praying right now, and what are we praying about?*

You wouldn't be engaged in prayer at that moment because there was no "on-ramp." There was nothing to take you from where you were, shopping with an agenda, to a place where your heart, mind, and body could engage in prayer.

Now, let's try that scenario again but with an on-ramp. This time, you see your friend coming toward you. "Hey! How's it going?" she asks. You answer with something boring because your mind is focused on what you need to buy. Next, you kindly ask how she's doing. You see the expression on her face change as she starts sharing about the struggle she and her husband are having with their son. She elaborates on how it's affected various areas of their life. Then with an expression of hope, she looks up and says, "Hey, would you mind praying with me in the parking lot when we're done here?"

"Oh, of course! I'll meet you out there in twenty minutes," you respond. Twenty minutes later, your shopping is done and you're outside praying with your friend. Now how engaged are you in prayer?

What changed? Your friend's situation is just as dire in scenario B as in scenario A. God is just as able to hear prayers and answer them in both scenarios. The difference is, in scenario B, *you* were ready. Your heart, mind, and body were prepared to go before the Father on behalf of your friend. In scenario B, you had an on-ramp that functioned to prepare you for prayer.

An on-ramp takes someone from where they are to a place where they are ready to engage with Jesus. Despite our best efforts, our children may often identify more with scenario A than B when we initiate prayer. What a shame. Prayer *can* be a powerful and intimate experience when one is *ready* to pray.

We could teach our children to do all the "right" outward things during prayer, but that's not our goal. Our hope is that they will talk to God with an honest and genuine heart. In order to point them in this direction, there are some simple things we can do that will function as an on-ramp for them to travel on *before* we start praying.

Building an On-Ramp

Throughout the Bible, we see people journey to meet with God. We see Moses climb Mount Sinai, we see Hannah journey to the temple, and we see people regularly make pilgrimages in order to pray and offer sacrifices to Him. Psalm 84:7 talks about enduring the journey just to see the Lord: "They go from strength to strength, till each appears before God in Zion" (NIV). In the New Testament, people were constantly journeying to meet with Jesus. Remember the paralyzed man who was lowered in front of Him through the roof? I wonder how far he journeyed to see Jesus.

While we need not make a long physical journey to speak to God today, there is still a journey to be made. When we initiate prayer, we are attempting to bring our children from wherever they are mentally, physically, and emotionally to a place where they are talking with God, a place where their bodies are ready, their hearts are engaged, and their minds are focused to meet with Him.

Before we get into how to construct an on-ramp, keep in mind that the ideas here are not designed to be used every time. Instead, pick a few that will fit the situation you're in, the time you have available, and what is realistic for your family. If you don't build an on-ramp, your children are less likely to be engaged, but build too much of a ramp and you risk the same problem.

> When we initiate prayer, we are attempting to bring our children from wherever they are mentally, physically, and emotionally to a place where they are talking with God.

Also, these ideas are not foolproof. No matter how good the ramp is, if your timing is poor or your child is melting down, it may all be in vain. The point is not to get our children to pray whenever *we* want but to help them engage in prayer more effectively.

Now let's look at how we can more mindfully construct an on-ramp for our children in order to help them fully engage in prayer. First, we will look at what I did to build an on-ramp in the opening story. Then we will look beyond that example at other ideas we can implement.

Gathering Your Children

The first thing I did after reading articles about the mistreatment of a minority group in China was to call the kids into the family room from their various activities. By doing this, I created a break in what they were doing and redirected their attention to something different. To be fair, time was on our side and not much was happening at that moment. If, however, there was a lot going on, I might have waited for a better time—maybe at bedtime, on a car ride, or after dinner when everyone was already together.

Yelling for everyone to stop what they're doing and "Come right now!" will not build an on-ramp; it will damage it. You don't have to test me on this. I know from experience. So be considerate in how you call them together. Think of it as inviting them, rather than commanding them, to do something together.

Setting the Environment

As I called all the kids into the family room, I pulled the green corduroy chair and the beanbag closer to the couch so we could all be cozy together. If you've ever sat with me for a conversation in my house, you've seen where I usually sit: the corner of the couch under the lamp with the giant white pillow. Well, mostly white—I have five kids after all. But on this occasion, I sat on the floor because I wanted to make sure everyone else was comfortable. If the TV had been on and a giant marble run was in the middle of the floor, I would've turned the TV off and shifted the run out of the way. Moving the chair and beanbag took little effort and zero forethought, but in shifting the furniture slightly, I set the environment and created a space that was conducive to prayer.

When we pray in my kids' room before bed, I usually pick up any stuffed animals and blankets that are on the floor. Sometimes I do the opposite and pile them up to make a snuggle spot in the corner.

During the eight days of Hanukkah and pretty much all of December, we like to turn the lights down after dinner and light candles.

> **Pro Tip:** Nothing sets the mood for focused prayer like candles. (On the flip side, closing my eyes when my children are near an open flame is admittedly nerve-racking!)

As we read in the last chapter, our prayers are often referred to as incense or a sweet aroma. Instead of any ol' candle, maybe light a certain candle or defuse a specific oil during times of prayer. This will help create very memorable experiences with prayer.

There are countless things we can do to set the environment, and you're probably thinking of some right now that will appeal to your children. Take some time now to write down those good ideas before you forget them.

Using Information

As everyone was getting settled, I began reading aloud the article I mentioned earlier. Since I had already read it myself, I skipped some parts that were either too intense for children or not as pertinent. When I was done, I looked at them. I could tell by the looks on their faces that they already got it, but I said it anyway: "This is wrong."

From simply hearing the story and the detail of the treatment of the people involved, they understood that what was happening was wrong. Because I read the article out loud, they now had all the information they needed. Their hearts were stirred, and they knew key details, including names and places. Even the younger ones heard enough to know something they could pray about.

Years ago, I was a part of the South Jersey House of Prayer. We met on Saturday nights in a square cement building that was an old state armory. The heat was inadequate, and there was no air conditioning. If you ever want people to show up to your prayer meeting, (1) don't call it a prayer meeting, and (2) don't hold it in a place like this.

On a monthly basis, we would pray for women and children who were being trafficked in different cities around the globe. Some nights, I would spend the entire hour praying for places and faces I'd only seen in my imagination. How was I able to do that? I had been given information.

Each month, an organization called Exodus Cry put out information about a specific city that had rampant human trafficking.

That information would tell us what human trafficking looked and sounded like, who a typical buyer was, who was typically for sale, and what the government was doing or not doing about it. Just facts really. Just information. But from that information, we were able to pray for hours and hours.

Oftentimes only a little information is needed to stir our hearts. For example, if I hear from my son, "Josiah is sad," that stirs my heart, but more information can tell me how I can put that stirring into action. "Someone told him they didn't like him and wanted him to go home." Well, now I know how to pray. I can pray for that child who was rude. I can pray that the Holy Spirit will help Josiah be confident that he is loved. I can pray that he will have the courage to play on the playground again. I can pray that those words will not find a place in his heart and mind, and lots more. You get the idea.

Any time you're going to pray for something or someone, take a minute to share information about it, pull up a photo of the person, get out a globe, or find the "street view" on your phone. Let your children know why this is important. Why is this worth our time and prayers? Even adults rarely jump into praying without information, so make sure kids know all they need to before getting started.

> **One more Pro Tip:** It's not good timing to share lots of information when everyone has their utensils in hand and a hot plate of food in front of them.

Ask Questions

After reading the article to my kids, I asked some simple but thought-provoking questions:

- How do you think you would feel if someone took you from your home and brought you someplace else?
- How would you feel if Mommy or Daddy were taken away?
- How do you think God feels about this?
- What could we pray for?

When we ask questions, we provoke our children to think critically. When we get them thinking critically, they come up with the substance of prayer. We don't even need to tell them what to pray for. We're letting them come up with it themselves.

In this situation, I intentionally asked questions that would help my kids think critically and empathize with those suffering. Another time, I knew from talking to friends that their seven-year-old son, Marcos, was nervous about his upcoming ear surgery. After gathering the kids together and giving them information about the surgery, I turned to Marcos and asked, "Are you a little nervous about the surgery?"

"Yeah."

Then, addressing the rest of the kids, I said, "Marcos is feeling a little nervous. What do you think we could pray for regarding his surgery?"

The kids were quick to suggest praying that he wouldn't be nervous.

"What else could we pray about regarding the surgery?"

"For the doctor to do well?"

"For his recovery?"

We chatted, going back and forth with questions and answers for two minutes at most. By the time we actually closed our eyes to pray, they already knew what they needed to pray about. I have been surprised many times by the kind of answers my children have come up with independently when I've asked questions first.

Physical Position

If I stopped by your house and we chatted at the door, we would both know the conversation was going to be quick and that we both had things to do. If, however, you invited me into your family room and put a teakettle of water on the stove, I'd likely get cozy on your couch. The physical position we are in is indicative of our intentions.

So, after discussing with my children all that was happening in China, I said, "You can sit on the couch or kneel—whatever position might help your mind stay focused while we pray." Each one of them changed their position in order to pray. It was a way for them to express *I'm not just resting here; I'm positioning my body to do something important.*

We're going to look at our physical position more in chapter 7, but for now, consider that giving our children the option of choosing a physical position in which to pray can be an important way to help them focus and engage.

Worship Music

As the kids were adjusting their positions, I put on some worship music. Music is another tool that can help shift our attention and create an atmosphere that encourages prayer.

Most pastors like to have a time of worship before a sermon. Among other things, it helps the congregation transition from their morning car ride full of bickering, scarfing down the last bit of cereal, and lectures about putting shoes in their proper place so you don't have to look for them in the morning. I'm sure I'm not the only one who needs to transition from the chaos before my heart and mind can respond to the pastor's message.

Worship music isn't just a transitionary tool though; more importantly, it properly postures our hearts before God. Rhythm and melody working together move us in a special way. For children and adults alike, I believe music calms our minds and helps focus the affections of our hearts on God. Of all the art forms God could've had around His throne, He chose songs, instruments, and praise.

Before having a time of prayer, consider playing or singing a song or two to help your children (and you) focus on God. My family loves songs that are easily sung a capella, like "Turn Your Eyes upon Jesus," "'Tis So Sweet to Trust in Jesus," and "Jesus Loves Me." What are some songs your children enjoy? Take a moment to write them down, and plan to sing one or two the next time you're going to pray together.

Visualization

When I was very little, my mother sat on the edge of my bed to comfort me because I was too scared to go to sleep. She told me a trick she used when she was a little girl. She said, "When I felt scared, I didn't just pray. I'd imagine God on His great throne with Jesus on a throne on one side and Mary on a throne on His other side." In case you were wondering, yes, my mother grew up Catholic.

Visualization is a powerful tool. Because many other religions and New Age practices use it as well, I would like to be extra clear here. I'm not talking about visualization in some mystical or metaphysical way. I'm talking about picturing in our minds what we know to be true from Scripture.

We have been given several pictures of God, His throne, His angels, and heaven. I have reminded my children of these pictures countless times. Why? Because, just like my mom's trick did for me, it helps them remember they are not just wishing on stars or lifting their voices up to the universe, hoping something somewhere hears and cares. They are talking to *God*; they can speak to His face when they pray. They are talking to the Maker of all things, the Creator of heaven and earth, the Lord of Lords, and King of Kings!

Next time you're about to pray, try picturing this scene from Revelation and see if it doesn't change the way you pray:

> Among the lampstands was one like the Son of Man, dressed in a robe and with a golden sash wrapped around his chest. The hair of his head was white as wool—white as snow—and his eyes like a fiery flame. His feet were like fine bronze as it is fired in a furnace, and his voice like the sound of cascading waters....

> He laid his right hand on me and said, "Don't
> be afraid. I am the First and the Last, and the
> Living One. I was dead, but look—I am alive for-
> ever and ever, and I hold the keys of death and
> Hades." (Rev. 1:13–15, 17b–18)

Why not try engaging your children with some visual stimuli from the Bible and see how it transforms their prayer time?

Remembering God's Character and Truth

In the previous chapter, we discussed the basics that every child should understand about prayer. Reminding our children of these truths at any ol' time is a good idea, but reminding them before praying is a great idea and helps them more effectively prepare their hearts for what they are about to do.

> "Remember, God hears our prayers."
> "God loves to hear your voice. Why don't you
>   pray this time?"
> "He loves it when we look to Him for things we
>   need."

A short, simple reminder of who they are praying to can make all the difference between your child bowing their head to pray because they're anxious to eat or being genuinely thankful for their food.

Part of teaching our children who God is means reminding them of what He has done. Oftentimes we see people recount what

God has already done before they pray and then ask God to do more. *God, who parted the seas, would You raise Your hand again to help us?*

When we remind our children what God has done in one situation, it gives them faith that He might act in a similar way. This is exactly what we read about in Matthew 4:24: "The news about him spread throughout Syria. So they brought to him all those who were afflicted.... And he healed them."

Upon hearing what Jesus had done, people had hope that He might do it again. They heard He healed others, so the sick came in faith that He would heal again. And He did! The same is true for us and our children. Whether we're drawing from our own experiences or from a story in the Bible, when we share a testimony of what God has done, it will increase our faith and our children's faith. We will talk more about the power of remembering and the role testimonies play in chapter 12.

  Part of teaching our children who God is means reminding them of what He has done.

Tradition and Routine

Suppose you invite your neighbors over for dinner. They are not Christians, but when you say, "Let's pray," they instinctively bow their heads and close their eyes. Why? Because of tradition. Though they don't practice prayer in their own lives, it's a custom they're familiar with. So familiar with that, in that moment, they didn't need instruction on what to do; they did it automatically.

Consistently praying at certain times will create a similar effect. When our children expect to pray, there will be fewer distractions for them to overcome and therefore less of a "journey" to be made.

Many parents express that praying before dinner and bed have become so expected it feels routine. They're concerned their children aren't engaging. Do you have this concern as well? My response is this: if praying before dinner or bed is a tradition, keep it up! You've established "planned" times of prayer. If prayer has become disingenuous, consider building more of an on-ramp or changing up what the prayer time looks like. We're going to talk all about that in the next couple of chapters.

Who's Building an On-Ramp for Who?

I've worked on being diligent with on-ramps and explaining why they're important for our kids, but this isn't just a lesson for *them*. After a long conversation with my daughter one day, I was feeling anxious to get on with my evening chores. As our talk seemed to wrap up, I started pushing myself up off her bed, but she quickly asked, "Well, will you pray with me about all that?" Whoops. Turns out she was building an on-ramp for *me*! I was about to walk away, feeling satisfied that we had talked through things; meanwhile, in her mind, we hadn't even reached the end goal—to pray about it.

The more accustomed our children get to an on-ramp, the easier it will be for them to slide into prayer. And even better, they will learn how to create an on-ramp for others. In the scenarios I presented earlier, it is assumed that we, the parents, are initiating prayer, but be sensitive to clues that your child may be building an on-ramp for you.

A common concern I hear from parents is that their children pray the same thing over and over. Now that we've created a solid on-ramp to bring our children from where they are to a place where they're ready to pray, let's discuss *what* we pray with them.

Chapter 6

WHAT TO PRAY

Beyond "God Bless This Food. Amen."

I made beautiful mugs, cups, and vases in my high school ceramics class. Although it was standard beginner stuff, looking back now, I realize it was pretty good. One piece I made actually won a spot in a local art show. I assumed I was just good with clay. *I must have natural talent!* Perhaps I had some talent, but most of the credit is due to my teacher.

It wasn't until years after my ceramics class that I realized just how great a teacher she was. When my husband and I and our three girls lived in New Jersey, I rented some space at a local ceramics studio for a brief time. Because it had been so long since I'd worked with clay, I decided to sign up for a couple of refresher classes. As these classes were full of adult students, we were given a lot more freedom. I experimented more with techniques and glazes, though I mostly made pieces similar to the ones I had made in high school: mugs, cups, and vases.

At Christmastime, I brought my best pieces home to my mom in New York. To my surprise, my latest pieces looked worse than the ones already sitting on her shelf from my high school years. By comparison, the ones I now held were thick, heavy, and hardly uniform. *What's the problem?* I felt frustrated as I stared at the pieces. *How is it that the work I did years ago in high school is so much better?*

After pondering the problem for a while, I figured it out. I was given specific instructions in my high school class. My teacher taught like an engineer. She shared a variety of techniques and demonstrated exactly how to perform those techniques, such as the right way to roll clay into a long coil. She showed us how to prepare the clay, mold it, slap it on the wheel, and then hold the mound until it was perfectly centered. I remember a few kids spending the whole class just trying to center their mound of clay on the wheel.

By comparison, the class I took in New Jersey had little instruction. The teacher emphasized feeling out the clay, working with it till it "felt right." I had an incredible amount of freedom; however, I lacked the skills I needed to make use of that freedom. Because I struggled with the basics, the freedom ended up being of little use to me, and worse, I couldn't make wonderful ceramics. It felt like someone brought me to a garage full of tools and supplies and said, "Here, make whatever you want," but never showed me how to use the different tools. Despite the freedom, I never made anything more than cups and vases, and all were worse than what I'd made years before.

We have an incredible amount of freedom in prayer; however, like my freedom in the ceramics class in New Jersey, much of it will be of little value without good instruction and will likely lead us to fall prey to ruts and stagnant routines.

How many times have you told your child, "You can pray whatever you want," but they pray the same thing they did the night before? Children often pray repetitively because they don't know what else to pray. This is not actually a problem, as we'll see in chapter 8 when we talk about the role persistence plays in prayer. But if we can expand *what* they pray, or the content of their prayer, they'll be able to make better use of all those wonderful tools and thrive in the freedom of prayer rather than get lost in it.

Just like learning how to use all that equipment in the garage, we're going to explore how to use different types of prayer and structures for prayer. Then we'll look at how we can use the greatest resource of all—the Bible. All this instruction will help our children pray with the power and potential God intended and expand the ways in which they connect with Him.

Types of Prayer

Throughout the Old and New Testament, we see people pray all kinds of prayers to God. Sometimes they praised God for His faithfulness, sometimes they begged God to rescue them, and sometimes they wailed and lamented. In order to expand our understanding of prayer, let's begin by exploring three common types of prayer we see in the Bible: praise and thanksgiving, confession and repentance, and requests and intercession. Then we'll look at an easy way we can bring these types of prayer together with a guiding structure.

Praise and Thanksgiving

> Enter his gates with thanksgiving
> and his courts with praise.
> Give thanks to him and bless his name.
> (Ps. 100:4)

 Praise is not obligatory; it is our natural response to being in God's presence and reflecting on His magnificence.

Remember when the Cowardly Lion stammered, stuttered, and ran away after barely seeing the Wizard? He traveled all the way to Oz to meet him, yet when faced with the Wizard's magnificence (though it was a facade), the lion was too overwhelmed to stay in his presence.

When Isaiah saw a vision of God robed in glory upon His throne, heard the seraphim singing, and felt the foundations shake, Isaiah's first utterances were, "Woe is me for I am ruined" (Isa. 6:5). I imagine he must have felt helplessly fragile standing before God.

How might *we* feel if we met face to face with God? Praise is not obligatory; it is our natural response to being in God's presence and reflecting on His magnificence.

Prayers of praise and thanksgiving declare who God is and express thanks for what He has done. When giving praise, the posture of our hearts is low, humble, and full of gratitude.

Nehemiah provides a perfect example of a prayer of praise and thanksgiving.

> "Stand up. Blessed be the LORD your God from
> everlasting to everlasting."

> Blessed be your glorious name,
> and may it be exalted above all blessing and
>   praise.
> You, LORD, are the only God.
> You created the heavens,
> the highest heavens with all their stars,
> the earth and all that is on it,
> the seas and all that is in them.
> You give life to all of them,
> and all the stars of heaven worship you.
> (Neh. 9:5b–6)

Confession and Repentance

> Let us draw near with a true heart in full assurance of faith, with our hearts sprinkled clean from an evil conscience and our bodies washed in pure water. (Heb. 10:22)

Confession means we admit our wrongs. Repentance—our decision to turn away from sin and turn to God—is the next step to take. Confession and repentance are how we practice the truth (from chapter 4) that God wants our hearts to be honest and clean.

Requests and Intercession

> Don't worry about anything, but in everything,
> through prayer and petition with thanksgiving,
> present your requests to God. (Phil. 4:6)

Rarely do people have trouble with this one. One of the main ways we relate to God is through requests. We ask God to give us wisdom, watch over us, protect us, provide for our needs, and a whole host of other things. When Jesus prayed, His request was "Give us this day our daily bread" (Matt. 6:11 ESV).

Oftentimes, parents get concerned that their children don't have more complex prayer lives. "Sweetie, there's more to prayer than just asking God for stuff." And that's true; there most definitely is. But before we direct our children away from their list of desires, let's take a moment to consider a couple of key things happening here.

First, when our children bring their requests to God, they are looking to and hopefully trusting in Him for what they need or desire. This is excellent! As children of God, we should always look to Him. In times of difficulty, the Israelites repeatedly turned to other things: a gold calf, false gods, a king, Egypt, and so on. The next time your child prays that they'll have a good day at preschool, take a moment to commend them for turning to God.

Second, turning to God with requests is the foundation of intercessory prayer. As our children grow and mature, in addition to showing them how to turn to God for their own needs, we can teach them how to turn to God for others' needs.

Praying for others' needs is called intercession. You probably interceded for your child before they were even born. You likely asked God to keep them healthy and strong and a whole host of things. When our children are still in the womb, we know they are not praying for themselves, so we, as their moms and dads, pray on their behalf.

 In addition to showing them how to turn to God for their own needs, we can teach them how to turn to God for others' needs.

Intercessory prayer is something our children can begin when they are very young. To help them understand this concept, we might begin by telling them why we, as their parents, pray for them. "We love you very much and want you to be strong and healthy and love God. So we've prayed for you since before you were even born." This will help them piece together the connection that because they are important to you, you pray for them.

From there, we can point out that they love and care about other people too. "Who do you love that you want to pray for?" They will probably say Mommy or Daddy, a sibling, or another relative. So we've set our children up to understand that we pray for people we love.

The next step will be to help our children see the importance of praying for people other than those *they* love, because God loves those people. "We can even pray for that man there because God loves him."

For younger children, what we've established so far is an adequate understanding of intercession, but for kids around eight and older, we'll want to expand on the importance of requests.

All our intercession, whether we're praying for our daughters or our country, is just an extension of Jesus' prayer for God's kingdom to come to earth. When Jesus interceded, He prayed, "Your kingdom come. Your will be done on earth as it is in heaven" (Matt. 6:10).

Jesus' prayer indicates that God's good and perfect will isn't always accomplished here on earth. Hence, we pray for God's will to be done. Earth is full of fighting, tears, pain, and brokenness. But the great news is, we have a role to play. God uses our prayers to change things.

Here's what you might say:

> Things are not perfect here on earth. When Adam and Eve sinned, it caused evil to enter the world, and it was no longer God's perfect place. So any time we see a person or a situation that is not right, we can pray like Jesus prayed. Maybe we can say, "God I pray that Your kingdom will come and

Your will would be done in our house like it is in
heaven" (see Matt. 6:10).

Once your child begins to notice all the brokenness around
them, they'll realize there is no end to the things we can pray for
here on earth. If that's the case, hang tight; we'll revisit the topic
of intercession in chapter 10 and discover a practical approach
to mapping out our requests to God that will help our children
tremendously.

We've looked closely at three different types of prayer. Now
let's integrate these types of prayer together into one guiding
structure.

Introducing Structure: Limericks and Jesus' Prayer

I used to hate writing poems. I thought it was silly how poetry was
frequently thought of as being romantic. To me it was random,
vague, and unclear. However, the day I learned about limericks
in fifth grade, I experienced a turning point in my relationship
with poetry. To my great delight, I discovered that poetry could
be humorous, even absurd. Limericks, which are typically silly,
follow a very simple structure. They are five lines long with an
aabba rhyming pattern. Here's the poem I wrote that day in fifth
grade about my gymnastics coach:

There once was a girl named Mandy.
She ate a lot of candy.

She got sugar high,
And thought she could fly,
And that was the end of Mandy.

I didn't appreciate poetry until I discovered this fun and easy structure. Once I discovered this arrangement, I had lots of fun with it. To help expand our children's experience with prayer and expose them to different types of prayer, we can introduce a structure. Better yet, we can model it after what Jesus prayed. When His disciples wanted to know how to pray, Jesus answered,

Pray then like this:

"Our Father in heaven,
hallowed be your name.
Your kingdom come,
your will be done,
    on earth as it is in heaven.
Give us this day our daily bread,
and forgive us our debts,
    as we also have forgiven our debtors.
And lead us not into temptation,
    but deliver us from evil." (Matt. 6:9–13 ESV)

This prayer is far from a limerick, but it does have a guiding structure. In Jesus' prayer we see Him praise God, intercede, make requests of God, and ask for forgiveness. Let's take all those elements and put them into an easy-to-remember acronym: PRAY

(Praise, Repent, Ask, Yield). Can't get easier than that. This acronym comes from Steve Pettit's book *How to Pray 30 Minutes a Day* and is modified slightly. Although the elements are in a different order than they are in Jesus' prayer, this acronym will walk us through the different types of prayer mentioned above.

Praise

> Our Father in heaven,
> hallowed be your name. (v. 9b ESV)

To get our children started, we can expand on what Jesus prayed. "Our Father, holy and glorious and powerful is Your name! May Your name be known far and wide, throughout the whole earth!"

Maybe ask your children, "What has God done that we can praise Him for?" Or "Who is God? What is He like? What makes Him so special?"

Repent

> Forgive us our debts,
> as we also have forgiven our debtors. (v. 12 ESV)

Leading your children in a prayer of repentance may be as simple as, "We confess that we have sinned against You. Forgive us for all the things we've done wrong."

You might try prompting your children by saying: "Let's take a minute to admit we did some things today that were wrong. Then we can ask God to forgive us." I leave space for my children to pray in their heads here so they can look at their hearts more honestly. For older children, we can include something along these lines: "How have we not been who God has called us to be? [By that I mean loving, kind, gracious, etc.] Let's ask Him to forgive us for that."

Ask

> Your kingdom come,
> your will be done,
>   on earth as it is in heaven.
> Give us this day our daily bread. (vv. 10–11 ESV)

Sometimes you may want to let your children ask whatever they want of God. Sometimes you may want to guide this time by leading them to intercede for something or someone in particular.

Remember, intercession is us pleading for God to move or act on behalf of another.

Try having your children take turns praying for each other, praying for a friend or family member, or perhaps praying for your congregation or city. My all-time favorite prompt is: "What do you think God wants to do in _____?" (e.g., our city, our church, our home, my heart, your heart).

Yield

Yielding in prayer isn't really a type of prayer but rather something we practice in prayer. Yielding has two parts. First, we yield our voices and thoughts to let God speak. Second, we yield our will to His.

We begin yielding by quieting our own voices and thoughts. You might say, "Okay, we're going to sit quietly for one minute so we can listen to God with our hearts and minds."

You or one of your children can then start the time of quiet by praying, "Now, God, open our ears to hear what You have to say. You know our thoughts and concerns from the day. Speak to us and encourage us now." It would be wise to avoid putting pressure on this time, but being intentional about listening to God is an important skill to develop. Remember our truth statement from chapter 4: God speaks to us. Sometimes God speaks to us through the Word or through a friend and sometimes through a feeling or thought from the Holy Spirit.

For the second part of yielding, we simply conclude our prayer time by declaring our trust in God. Like what Jesus prayed before His death, we close with "Not our will but Your will be done." Here, we are declaring that we have put all our trust and hope in God first, foremost, and alone. And now we are practicing the truth that we can trust God with everything.

What I love about letting the PRAY acronym guide our prayers is that we can use it every time and our prayers can still be very different. How we pray, who we pray for, and what we pray for change each time. Typically, I assign a letter to each of my children and let them lead that part of the prayer. Or if we're short on time, we might each take a turn on praise, someone will close with a quick yielding prayer, and then we'll be done. As your family gets the hang of this, it will likely become your go-to guide for family prayer time.

The Bible as Our Guide

If my son Josiah ever prays for you, he will likely put his hand on your shoulder and, among other things, pray for you to "be strong and courageous." It will be very sweet but also powerful. He'll pray this for you because years ago he memorized Deuteronomy 31:6, which reads, "Be strong and courageous; don't be terrified or afraid of them. For the LORD your God is the one who will go with you; he will not leave you or abandon you." This verse must have made an impression on him because he uses it often when he prays for others.

We cannot talk about prayer without discussing how Scripture can help us pray. When we teach our children how to pray from verses, passages, or stories, we are taking the pressure off them to come up with their own original words and equipping them with God's words and godly ideas.

This isn't a new concept; all over the Bible, we see people pray *from* the Bible. In the book of Acts, believers prayed the words of Psalm 2:

> Master, you are the one who made the heaven, the
> earth, and the sea, and everything in them. You
> said through the Holy Spirit, by the mouth of our
> father David your servant:
>   Why do the Gentiles rage
>   and the peoples plot futile things?
>   The kings of the earth take their stand
>   and the rulers assemble together
>   against the Lord and against his Messiah.
>   (Acts 4:24b–26)

Teaching Our Children How to Pray from Scripture

Now, how do we actually help our children pray in this way? For starters, anytime you're listening to a sermon or reading the Bible, ask the Holy Spirit to highlight verses or passages for you. Here's a verse that stood out to me when I first started this practice:

> True instruction was in his mouth, and nothing wrong was found on his lips. He walked with me in peace and integrity and turned many from iniquity. (Mal. 2:6)

What a great verse! We can pray that nothing false would be found on our children's lips but that they would walk with God in peace and integrity and turn many from sin. Don't you just want to pray that for your children now? Go ahead. I'll be right here when you're done.

If a verse stands out to you, first pause to consider the passage, chapter, and book as a whole. Sometimes a verse sounds nice and fun, but in context, it doesn't mean quite what you thought it did at first. On the flip side, some verses aren't inspiring unless you understand the entire story.

Some books of the Bible are a little more "prayable" than others. Your highlighter cap might stay on during your read through Leviticus, but you won't be able to put it on during the Psalms.

When you come across a good verse for praying, highlight it and write it down. You might want to include a bit of the context too if you think you might forget. You could store these verses in a journal or in the notes section of your phone.

Next, be on the lookout for an opportune time to introduce the concept of praying the Bible. Maybe at the dinner table or before bed when your children want to pray for someone but aren't too sure what to pray. Here's what you might say:

> Have you ever wanted to pray for yourself or Grandma or a friend but weren't sure what to pray? There is so much we could pray, but sometimes it's hard to think of anything beyond "God, help them." Well, the Bible can help us pray for ourselves and others. And most importantly, the Bible shows us what kinds of things are important to God. Let me give you an example.
>
> This morning I read from 1 Samuel, where the priest, Samuel, is about to pick the new king of Israel. Naturally, he was looking for the biggest and strongest man, but God wanted a king who would love and follow Him. This is what the Bible said: "The LORD said to Samuel, 'Do not look at his appearance … for humans see what is visible, but the LORD sees the heart'" (1 Sam. 16:7).
>
> We have a tendency to assume things about people based on their appearance, like Samuel did. This verse is something we can pray for ourselves or others so we might look at people more like God does. We can pray straight from the verse,

"God, I pray that we would not look at people's outward appearance, but I pray we would look at their hearts instead."

Of course, we as parents don't always have to provide the verses. Encourage your children to write down the verses they find in a special spot, like a journal: "When you hear a verse at church or come across one in your Bible, be sure to write it down and use it to pray from." (In the appendix I've included a list of some great verses to get you started.)

In addition to verses, we might use people or concepts as a springboard for our prayers. Remember the strong tree from Jeremiah 17? We can pray using that verse as our inspiration: "God, I ask that my children be like strong trees, with such rooted trust in You that they are able to withstand the various storms of life."

People in the Bible can inspire our prayers also. While praying for me, someone once referred to me as Ruth. Thankfully, I realized what they were doing before I spoke up to say, "Excuse me, my name is actually Erica." They were using the book of Ruth to pray the qualities of Ruth over me. And after learning about the brave shepherd boy David, we might incorporate that into our prayer time. "Let's pray that we will be like David—courageous and having lots of trust in God."

As we practice incorporating verses, passages, and concepts into our prayers, our children will naturally begin doing this on their own. It will be as if they have learned a new language when it comes to prayer. Likely, the next time they come across a good verse, they'll be excited to share it with you!

Written Prayers

As a young child, I recited many prayers. One of my favorites was a dinner blessing we said together as a family. I prayed along with my parents and older siblings:

> God is great. God is good.
> Lettuce thank Him for our food.
> Bias hands we all are fed.
> Give us, Lord, our daily bread.

I figured bread and "lettuce" represented staple foods we should be thankful for with our "bias" hands. Though I didn't get all the words right, the prayer was still meaningful. My heart spoke with genuine thanks to God while my mouth spoke the words. In fact, in some ways I found it easier to be genuinely thankful because I wasn't distracted trying to come up with the words to pray.

When helping our children seek God in prayer, we might consider introducing them to written or liturgical prayers. Similar to how a greeting card seems to say just the right thing or how the words of a worship song can help guide our hearts, a written prayer can help ensure our children won't be hung up on what to pray, allowing them to immediately connect with God. Contrary to many preconceived ideas, writing out prayers for your children, using a book of prayers, or guiding them to write their own prayers may be deeply meaningful.

Perhaps you have one child who tends to wake up at night. Writing a prayer for her to recite when she's scared will help guide her directly to Jesus. Is there something your child struggles with on a regular basis? Consider writing a simple prayer for them—maybe a prayer they can pray before school or before going to bed.

When writing a prayer to be recited, keep it very simple—just a few lines—and consider using a rhyming pattern. One woman I spoke with recently wrote a prayer for her children to the tune of "Twinkle, Twinkle, Little Star."

What a special gift to give your children—a beautiful prayer written just for them, something they can recite and remember for years to come. They may even pass on some of the prayers to their own children!

All right, we've covered a lot! If you've read this far, you may have thought, *Erica, this is all fine and good, but my kids don't even sit still.* Don't worry—that's where we're headed next. We've thoroughly discussed the content of prayer. Now let's talk about what prayer can *look* like.

WHAT PRAYER CAN LOOK LIKE

"But They Won't Sit Still!"

What comes to mind when you think of someone in deep, mature prayer? Do you picture them kneeling at an altar? Maybe you imagine a small group of believers praying in a circle. Perhaps you picture a grandma who kneels at her bed every morning and prays for hours. Likely, whatever the image is, whether they are sitting, kneeling, or standing, the person or people who are praying are still.

Now think about the times *you* pray. When do you pray? What are you doing, and where are you? In all those times of prayer, how often are you motionless? Mmm. Probably not too often.

What is it about praying while being still that makes us think it's superior to and more mature than praying on the go?

Being still has value, for sure. When we aren't moving around, we're less likely to be distracted and better able to give God our full attention. Also, doesn't it seem appropriate that when we speak to the God of the universe, we set aside all other activities in order to pray and think only of Him?

As valuable as being still is, if we approach prayer with our children as if keeping our bodies from moving is the *only* way to pray, we'll likely hinder their ability to meet and connect with Jesus and inadvertently communicate that prayer is something only adults are capable of. We'll take this beautiful thing called prayer and set it up high on the shelf next to our precious china. In their minds, prayer will be labeled "Not for Children." If you're like me, you may have unintentionally done this in the way you pray with your children, talk about prayer, and expect them to pray.

What would it look like to take prayer off the china shelf and hand it to your children? Your sticky-fingered youngest, your rowdy middle child, and your couldn't-care-less oldest?

Don't get flustered. I know what you're thinking: *Their hands are dirty. They're going to run around the house with it. They don't even appreciate how valuable it is!* Translation: *What about having reverence and awe in prayer? Is it too much to ask to have the children sit still?*

These are all great questions. In fact, the disciples had similar concerns when they saw all the people crowding around Jesus with their messy babies and loud kids. Matthew, Mark, and Luke all record the disciples' response: they "rebuked" the people (Matt. 19:13; Mark 10:13; Luke 18:15).

But Jesus had a different idea. He said, "Let the little children come to me and do not hinder them, for to such *belongs* the kingdom of heaven" (Matt 19:14 ESV). As parents, grandparents, caregivers, and teachers, we want to be the people bringing the children to Jesus, not the disciples who wanted to keep them back. We want to get right on their level and show them this beautiful thing called prayer.

 What would it look like to take prayer off the china shelf and hand it to your children?

Because we've established that stillness has value, we won't throw it out the window, but we *will* put it in its proper place. Being still is not the *goal* in prayer. Our goal is to initiate times that our children can meaningfully and genuinely communicate with God. Being still is simply *a way* in which that can happen, not *the* way.

It's an excellent idea to practice stillness with our children and expand their ability to sit still. However, think about being still. What do we value about it? More than the stillness itself, we value giving God our full and undivided attention. So rather than making stillness the ideal, we are going to focus on ways we can grow our children's ability to give God their full and undivided attention. As you'll see, sometimes keeping our bodies moving will not only help our children to focus on God longer, but it may be the best way for them to express their prayers.

Now let's go back to all those times you pray throughout the day without giving God your full attention. Maybe you're multitasking at work. Maybe you're silently calling, *Lord, help me!*

while listening to your daughter complain. Been there! Are those times less valuable because you cannot give God your full attention? Should we only pray when we can give God our full and motionless attention? No, of course not.

The value of praying on the go is that we bring Jesus into our daily lives. Well, we're not bringing Him in as much as we are acknowledging His presence with us. Praying on the go means we look to Him throughout the day in everything we do. Sounds pretty beautiful, doesn't it? Don't we want that for our children too?

With all that in mind, we have two goals as we approach this chapter: First, we want to expand our children's ability to focus on God. Second, we want to show them we can talk to Jesus throughout the day, even in our activities and play. By the end of this chapter, you'll have a toolbox full of ideas for what prayer can look like for your family.

Physically Engaging in Prayer

I remember hearing someone in my youth group say that the key to staying focused while praying is to write out your prayers. Really? Getting distracted was a huge problem of mine. I wanted to pray, but my prayers quickly turned into wondering what I was going to wear the next day and who I was going to talk with on the bus.

At the advice of a peer, I began writing out my prayers. And guess what—it worked. All those journals I flipped through years after high school were a result of adopting this method to help me focus in prayer.

What is it about writing prayers out on paper that helps us focus? The science behind it is quite fascinating. It turns out that when your hand moves on the paper, your brain does such and such and blah, blah, blah. Sorry, I don't know the science of it. What I *can* tell you is my hypothesis: after years of informal field "research," I think the reason writing our prayers increases our ability to focus is because physically interacting with what our minds are thinking about *reinforces* and *encourages* that work.

How about we conduct our own experiment right here? Stay right where you are. Don't move. See how long you can think about triangles. All kinds of triangles. Ready? Go.

How long were you able to think about triangles? Now, let's try this again, but first grab a piece of paper and a pen and see how long you can think about triangles while you draw them: big ones, little ones, right triangles, obtuse triangles, ones that look like pizzas ...

How long were you able to think about triangles this time? Okay, I doubt you actually did the experiment, but if you had, I'm sure you would've discovered that you could think about triangles for a surprisingly long time. Here's the best part: though your thoughts may have wandered here or there, you kept coming back to triangles because your body was physically interacting with your thoughts. *Physically* engaging in our prayers lengthens our *mental* engagement as well.

If this is true for "mature" adults, it's especially true for children. When I conducted this experiment with my children years ago, they were all amazed at how long they could think about something as random as triangles just because they were drawing them.

Praying involves our hearts, minds, and souls, which means our children can do just about anything and still pray. But rather than encouraging random motion, we're going to look at some movements our children can do with the intent of helping them engage longer and more fully in prayer. After we look at ways our children can physically engage, we'll switch gears and look at ideas for helping them practice stillness and focus in prayer.

Using Hands

No matter how rowdy a room of Sunday school kids is, I can command their attention with two words: "Simon says." Each child will drop what they're doing and listen intently so as not to lose the game. This first idea takes a cue from Simon Says: we simply place our hands on different areas of our bodies as a way of directing our prayers.

Suppose you're going to pray with a class full of kids or your child before bed. You could say, "Okay, let's pray for our bodies before bed. Follow my motions as you pray with me. Put your hands on your head." Then directing your words to God, you'd pray for your minds, "God, we ask You to give us wisdom and understanding."

"Now let's pray for our ears. Put your hands on your ears." Once you and the children move your hands to your ears, you'd pray, "God, would You make us good listeners? Help us to not only listen well to those around us but to also hear Your voice and guidance."

Then continue praying in this way for different areas of your body. Here are some ideas:

> **Eyes:** Pray for healthy eyes, that we would see people the way God sees them and see ourselves the way He sees us.

> **Mouth:** Pray to use our mouths for good, that we would speak only truth and our words would encourage others, not hurt them.

> **Hands:** Pray to use our hands for good, that we would help others with our hands and that the work we do with them would be pleasing to God.

> **Feet/legs:** Pray for God's Word to light our way, that we would avoid places we're not supposed to go and know that wherever we go, God goes with us.

> **Belly:** Pray to be healthy, active, and healed from our sicknesses and diseases and that we would make wise choices for what to eat.

> **Heart:** Pray that we would love God with all our hearts and love others as ourselves.

With this technique, children are not only interacting with their prayers and thinking critically about what's important for their bodies, but they are also considering their actions as they relate to God's plans and purposes for them.

Outside-the-Box Motion

One evening before bed, I was attempting to pray with two of my children. They were so rowdy, I wasn't sure how it was going to work. Not having the patience to build an on-ramp for them and knowing how occupied they were in their activity, I decided to bring prayer into what they were already doing. The only trouble was they were taking turns rolling off the bed. *How is this going to work?*

"Okay, okay." I put my hand on my daughter to pause her from rolling off. "This time, before you roll off, you need to tell God one thing you're thankful for." "I'm thankful for my family!" she proclaimed while rolling. My son anxiously climbed up next, shouted his thanks, and rolled. They proceeded to do this for quite a while. Was this a reverent time of prayer? Well, no. Were they in awe of God while they prayed? Doubtful. But did they learn that they can connect with God even in their play? Yes. I'm sure they did.

Rolling off the bed is sort of a bizarre way to engage in prayer. But it's good to keep in mind that many repetitive activities can be used to engage or extend our prayers.

Take running for example. Though it seems odd, children can pray while they run. In fact, exercise can be very good for helping the brain think clearly. What if your child needs to run? You can say, "How about you run around the house and for each lap, pray for one person for the duration of the lap?" If I prompted my son to pray for his friends before bed, he would pray for fifteen seconds. However, if he is running laps around the house and praying for a friend during each lap, he will be more intentional with his thoughts and praying the length of each lap. Might his mind wander a bit? Sure, but not any more than it would wander if he were just sitting in his room. And because he's running "prayer laps," as soon as he remembers what he's doing, his thoughts will go back to prayer.

Is your child active? Consider thinking creatively about how you might be able to introduce prayer into what they already like to do.

Walking, Pacing, and Rocking

Growing up, it was obvious when my brother was excited about what he was sharing. While my mom stood at the kitchen sink listening, he would talk on and on, oblivious to the circle he was wearing in the floor. If anyone mentioned his pacing, he got sidetracked and frustrated over the interruption. His physical movement was just an expression of the excitement in his mind. It was as if he was able to let out all that was on his mind in the form of pacing.

I wasn't surprised the first time I saw the way men prayed at the Western Wall. Jerusalem's Western Wall, also called the Wailing Wall, is a remnant of the wall that surrounded the first and second temples. Many people visit it to pray and recite prayers. All along the wall, people are rocking gently back and forth, pacing, standing, sitting, reading out loud, and using their hands in various ways as they pray.

When my children walk by my bedroom and see me sitting on my bed rocking, they know I'm praying. I don't need to rock, but I'm expressing with my body the urgency my heart feels, as though rocking were the natural response to the fire within me. On the other hand, there are plenty of times I feel distracted and apathetic, but rocking is my way of speaking to my heart, *Wake up! Get on board and intercede for the things of God's kingdom.*

While praying or interceding, a steady motion can feel very fitting. It may seem odd, but letting our children know they can walk around, rock, or even sway when they pray may be extremely helpful. Sometimes sitting still just doesn't fit with the energy we have inside. There may be times children have a lot on their minds to talk with God about, and this motion may help them let out all those thoughts.

Additionally, perhaps you want to plan to walk and pray together. Many families, small groups, and congregations do what's called "prayer walking." The idea is simple: you walk around a school, a neighborhood, your church building, or another location and intercede for it while you walk. This form of praying not only invites a steady motion, but it also brings our prayers on-site, which can intensify our desire to pray.

Crafts: Keeping Hands Busy

This past summer, two of my children learned to whittle. I got them a simple kit for beginners, they found some sticks, and they started whittling away. Surprisingly, they made a dolphin and a bird-ish form. I tried to make a spinning top, but it turns out that a perfectly symmetrical object doesn't make a good beginner project.

I often suggest they pull out their knives and a piece of wood and whittle over a cookie sheet when I need to read a lot to them for school. Unfortunately, the cookie sheet only catches about half the mess, but it's worth it because I can read several chapters at a time and they don't complain. Working with their hands enables them to sit and listen longer, which is how this skill can be applied to prayer time. The good news is that keeping children's hands occupied doesn't have to involve a mess and the potential for blood.

There are many interactive things our children can do with their hands that won't be too distracting while they pray. If you're in a situation where you'd like your children to be still, such as a prayer service or something similar, ask yourself, *Is there something my daughter can do that's not too messy or distracting but will still allow her a chance to move her hands?*

Suggest that your child's project become one giant prayer—praying with every stitch, knit, or purl for the person they are making it for.

Things that work well are Play-Doh (just one color, though, and hold off on any tools), a piece of clay, or even a slice of beeswax. (Beeswax has a nice scent to it, and it has to warm up in your child's hands before it becomes malleable.) Any of these may be an excellent way to make prayer a sensory experience. These moldable materials could also serve to reinforce their prayers. "How about you play with this while you're praying? Then when you're done, you'll have a creation made from your prayers: a prayer creation!"

Do any of your older children enjoy knitting, crocheting, sewing by hand, embroidery work, friendship bracelets, and the like? These projects can be great things to associate with prayer. Additionally, you might suggest that your child's project become one giant prayer—praying with every stitch, knit, or purl for the person they are making it for.

Stick Figure Drawings

I can still remember watching my mother draw in the corners of her bulletin during the sermon on Sundays. She had a way of creating faces and figures that captivated me. They were hardly more than doodles, but I loved them. I never grew out of stick figure drawings. They are still my style of choice when drawing. But more importantly, we can use the simplest of stick figures to pull our children into prayer.

The other day I was sitting at the table with my two boys when I got word that my brother-in-law was still in the hospital struggling with COVID-19. Knowing it was a matter of seconds before they finished their last bite of cereal and began running around, I quickly grabbed a piece of paper and slapped it on the table between them. "Hey, we are going to pray for Uncle Manny before we move on." Before I finished the sentence, I had already drawn a stick figure lying on a bed. "This is Uncle Manny at the hospital. We can pray for God to heal his lungs and heart." I drew a heart on him and two ovals as lungs.

The boys' eyes followed my pencil as I drew two other stick figures standing. "These are his nurse and his doctor. We can pray for them to have wisdom and to care for Uncle Manny well." On the other side of Stick Figure Manny, I drew a fourth person, his wife. "This is Aunt Michelle. We can pray for her to not get tired or worn out but to have hope and energy to keep visiting him and caring for everyone else." Then I drew a pathetic rendering of what I called "equipment"—squiggly lines and squares—around his bed.

Putting my pencil down and looking up at them I said, "Okay, who wants to pray for Uncle Manny?" My boys and I took turns praying for everyone in the room, placing our pointer finger on whichever person we were praying for. Because I had drawn out what we were praying for, the boys were able to engage more. We could have prayed *while* I drew too, instead of praying when the picture was all done.

It might be hard for your child to really engage in praying for things outside their world. But what if you pulled out a piece of paper, drew a rectangle building with a cross on top, and said, "What do you think God wants to do in our church?" Then, whatever they said, you could do a little drawing to go along with it. On the next page is an example of a stick figure drawing for a church.

Once you and your children get the hang of this, there's no limit to the kinds of things you might think to draw while you're praying!

Drawing, Coloring, and Journaling

Years ago, I spoke at a mother-daughter retreat. Following one of the sessions, a mother came up for prayer. As we were finishing, her daughter walked over. I'm pretty sure she came over to get her mom, but I wasn't going to pass up a chance to pray for the daughter too.

While praying for the daughter, a picture came to mind. I saw an image of a hand on paper holding a pencil. I paused my prayer to ask her, "Are you pretty creative? Like do you like to write?" She shook her head. "No, not really." Her mom interjected, "Well, she doesn't like to write, but she is creative." Turning to her daughter, she said, "Show her your notebook." She showed me several of her sketches, and it was clear she was excellent at drawing! When I saw an image of a hand on paper, my mind assumed it was writing. She was creative, just not with words as I had first thought.

I believe the Holy Spirit showed me this image for several reasons. He wanted me to encourage her love of drawing and for her to know this gift was from Him and that He was delighted in her ability to draw. Additionally, I believe He wanted her to begin to see her drawing as a way in which she could connect with God. As I continued praying, I praised God for the gift He had given her and asked that it be a special way for her to connect with Him.

Coloring, drawing, or journaling may be great ways for your children to interact with their prayers. Drawing can become an alternative to speaking their prayers out loud. You can say something like: "How about we spend a little time thanking God for His blessings? You can write or draw the things you're thankful for. Think of your drawings as your prayers."

Sometimes you may just hand your children some paper and a crayon. Other times, why not break out all your art supplies, play worship music, and let them create something on butcher paper or a large canvas while praying? Maybe you have some scrap plywood or some large rocks outside. All these things could be painted as an expression of our prayers.

As we've discussed, writing out our prayers can help keep us focused. Why not encourage your children to pull out their journals and pray? Tell them it will not only help them stay focused, but they'll also be able to look back over the things they prayed about and praise God for all He's done! (More on journals in chapter 10.)

More!

In case I haven't given you enough ideas already, here are additional ways we can help our children physically engage in prayer:

- Pull out a map or globe, and have children place their fingers/hands on the region as they pray.
- Draw a chalk outline of a place, person, name, building, or other object, and have children color it in while praying. Or, instead of using chalk on the sidewalk, use finger paint and a sheet of paper.

- Pray for someone in need while collecting flowers. All the flowers in the vase represent your prayers. When you pass by them, it'll be a reminder to pray for that person. When it's time to pick new flowers, pray for someone or something different.
- Build a structure or tower with toy blocks. Take turns praying every time you add a block.
- Build a family rock cairn. Each rock can represent a special prayer or verse prayed for a family member.
- Use each of your fingers as prayer prompts. Pope Francis has an excellent guide for this![1]

Being Still

We've discussed many ways that movement can help our children pray. There is also a place for stillness. Whether it's sitting around the table, snuggling on the couch, or sitting at a service, there are times that sitting still makes the most sense. Being still and focused in prayer is hard even for adults, so here are some ways to help your kids develop this ability.

> **Start when they are young.** For whatever reason, our children did not begin going into children's ministry classrooms during Sunday service until they were five or older, if at all. That additional time with us proved to be a perfect chance to practice sitting still and being quiet. Since we began when

they were babies, it wasn't a big deal for them to sit either on our laps or on the seat next to us. That's not to say it wasn't without its struggles; we had to be consistent and creative. And there were many weeks we listened to the sermon from the lobby. Just because our kids were sitting and attempting to be quiet didn't mean nothing else was going on. I would often hold their attention by drawing little stick figures on a piece of paper (passing on the tradition), sometimes even drawing out the stories our pastor told.

Build a solid on-ramp. This step is *huge*. (Refer to chapter 5 for ideas on this.) Remember, the more effort you put into preparing your children to pray, the more ready they will be to actually pray.

Communicate why you're asking them to be still and the value of it. Is it because you want to develop your children's ability to be still in prayer? Is stillness appropriate because of the circumstances or environment? Is it because of what you're praying about (i.e., a serious and heavy issue)? In words they will understand, communicate that sometimes we stop everything to give God all our attention. They should understand something to the effect of, "I'm not doing other things right now so I can focus all my attention on God."

Communicate how long you expect them to sit still. To the best of your knowledge, how long will this prayer time last? If your child is antsy, asking them to be still for thirty minutes is probably unrealistic, but five minutes may be doable. Find the balance in what you're asking so you can set them up to succeed but still stretch them a little.

We've probably all heard that it's a good idea to introduce lots of fruits and vegetables to our children when they're young so they become accustomed to a wide range of healthy foods. Think of using this same approach when expanding your children's prayer "palate." When you first try a new idea, it may feel awkward, but the more you do it, the more it will become a natural part of prayer.

As our children grow, they'll decide which things to continue on their own as part of their prayer lives. Someday when they're in college and running for their school, they might not be able to help but talk to God with every stride. Maybe they'll knit a hundred blankets in their lifetime, all representing prayers for others or praise to God. The ideas we introduce now will serve our children for many years to come!

HOW WE PRAY

Five Qualities of the Heart

Imagine for a moment that you're putting your daughter to bed. She's got her comfiest jammies on, and all the lights in her room are off except for her favorite star night-light in the corner. You pull the sheets up just under her chin and sit on the edge of her bed. Before you pray with her you ask, "What was your favorite part of today?" After she shares about her time on the playground laughing with friends, you begin to imagine all the encounters she'll have, the lessons she'll learn, and the life she'll experience. Feeling a weight of responsibility for your innocent little girl, you realize you don't just want to pray with her, you want to encourage her heart. You want to awaken her to the beauty of prayer and impress upon her, even at this young age, how to posture her heart for powerful, effective conversation with God.

Up to this point, we've learned different methods and techniques to help our children pray, but now is a good time to pause in our discussion of practical steps and look a little deeper into the heart qualities we desire our children to have as they come to their Father in prayer.

If you or I wanted to improve our prayer lives, we'd likely opt for a new routine, a different approach, or clearer goals, but probably all that would really need to change is our heart attitude toward prayer. In fact, even if we had no routine, no approach, and zero goals, I'm certain our prayer lives would improve drastically if we only focused more intentionally on our hearts.

The Bible talks about many qualities of prayer: some are *ways* we can pray (e.g., fervently, earnestly, persistently), some are *attitudes* we can have when praying (e.g., humbly, reverently, hopefully), and others are *actions* we can take in prayer (e.g., bowing, obeying, fasting). In this chapter we're going to cover just five: faith, persistence, reverence, humility, and fasting.

To help us better understand these vital qualities ourselves and how to talk about them with our children, each of the following sections begins with a paraphrased story from Scripture, followed by a "Simplifying" section that breaks the concept down even further. Parents of younger children may find this particularly helpful.

1. Faith

> Let him ask in faith without doubting. For the doubter is like the surging sea, driven and tossed by the wind. (James 1:6)

> There were three young men who loved and served God. Unfortunately, they worked for a king who did not. One day, the king was throwing a celebration,

and as part of the celebration, he declared that when the music began, everyone was to bow down and worship a large gold statue he had made. But when the music started, the three young men who loved and served God remained standing.

The king was furious about this, but he gave them a second chance saying, "This time, when you hear the music, you are to bow down and worship the gold statue I set up. If you don't, you'll be thrown into a furnace of fire."

But the men replied, "Our God is more powerful than you and can rescue us! But even if He doesn't rescue us, we will never worship the gold statue you set up."

Filled with rage because of the men's refusal, the king had the three men thrown into a furnace of blazing fire. But God protected them. When the king looked into the large furnace, he saw *four* men walking around and not harmed at all. (See Dan. 3.)

These men had impressive faith! They were so devoted to God and so confident that God could save them that they refused to bow down to the statue.

Having faith means we believe that God is who He says He is, will do what He has said He will do, and can do all things. Because of this, we trust Him completely. I love this story about Shadrach, Meshach, and Abednego because they had great faith, knowing what God *could* do, but they admitted they weren't sure what He *would* do. When we think of faith in regard to prayer, sometimes we assume that having faith means we are sure of what God will do. But faith is having assurance of what God *can* do, even though we don't always know what He *will* do.

Our children's faith can sometimes be shaken if God doesn't answer a prayer in the way they hoped. While situations like that can certainly feel discouraging, we can remind them that praying with faith (certainty about what God *can* do) is what God calls us to do. We must leave the rest up to Him.

We might also discuss that faith often leads to action. We not only pray with faith, but *because* of our faith, we obey God and do what is right even when we're not sure how things will work out. It was Shadrach, Meshach, and Abednego's faith that led them to obey even though the situation looked deadly.

Simplifying Faith

All children have been carried at some point. Even older children probably have some recollection of being carried when they were younger. Likely, they were picked up and brought somewhere and never thought twice about being dropped. This is a very relatable, real-life example to help them understand the concept of trusting God with the outcomes of their prayers.

> Can you remember a time you were carried? When you were carried, were you afraid Daddy might

drop you? Of course not. Daddy would never drop
you; he's plenty strong enough to carry you! You
might not have known where he was carrying you,
but likely you never questioned whether he could
carry you.

When we pray with faith, it means we have the
same confidence we had when we were carried.
It's as if we place our prayers in God's hands and
know for sure that God will not drop or ignore
our prayers. He hears and sees and can do or
carry anything. The Bible says He can even move
mountains!

Just as we trust our dads to carry us as children, we don't always know where God is carrying
us, but we have no doubt He can and will carry us
to a good place! When we pray with faith, we trust
His love for us and His power to handle all things.

2. Persistence

He told them a parable on the need for them to
pray always and not give up. (Luke 18:1)

There was once a man who was a judge for his
whole town. He didn't care what other people
thought of him, and, even worse, he didn't care
about God or doing what was right. One day a
woman came to him. She explained to the judge
that since her husband died, someone had been

treating her wrongly and she wanted the judge to help her. The judge didn't listen. Instead, he sent her away. The next day she came with the same plea. But the judge ignored her again. The woman kept coming back, day after day after day.

Even though the judge was not caring, he finally helped the woman so that she would stop bothering him. (See Luke 18:2–5.)

Jesus told this story to His disciples to encourage them to pray with the same persistence that this woman had when she visited the judge day after day. God wants us to pray with persistence, to keep asking and not give up our hope. We can remind our children that though the judge was not kindhearted, like God is, and didn't care about right and wrong, as God does, he gave her what she wanted because she wouldn't leave him alone. God is obviously much kinder than the judge, and when God sees our persistent faith, He will respond. The faith and persistence of the widow encourages us to be persistent.

Before sharing this story, Jesus had been talking with the disciples about His second coming. He went from describing the mysterious events preceding His return to telling a story about a widow. Seems kind of random, huh? But Luke 18:1 tells us why. It reads, "He told them a parable on the need for them to pray always and not give up." Knowing that life would be difficult and trying in the season He returned, Jesus wanted to prepare His disciples for the coming discouragement.

We can help our children build faith, and increase our own, by practicing persistence in prayer now.

Persistence, similar to perseverance, is what we choose to do when we begin to feel discouraged. In the season of Christ's return, we will be tempted to let discouragement keep us from seeking God. No matter where we are on the timeline of Christ's return, we will all experience seasons of difficulty and discouragement, but we can help our children build faith, and increase our own, by practicing persistence in prayer now.

Simplifying Persistence

Children know what it is to be annoying. Either they are the annoying one or someone else has annoyed them. The common factor is the persistence with which children do things: they *keep* asking, they *keep* interrupting, they *keep* throwing that ball. Inevitably, someone will burst out, "Stop doing that!"

When we talk to our children about persistence, we don't want to encourage annoying behavior, but we can use that as an example of God wanting us to *keep* praying.

> Mommy and I can get frustrated when you ask us over and over again, but God doesn't. In fact, He says that when we pray, we should ask over and over again and not give up asking. When we don't

give up on something, that's called being persistent. We should pray with persistence—or keep asking.

When we see our children getting discouraged, we can remind them to pray with persistence. It would be wise to incorporate some age-appropriate theology here. Persistence comes as a result of our faith in God, not of our own will or personal determination. Praying over and over and over again for selfish reasons will not convince God. Additionally, we should always have a heart attitude of *not my will but Your will be done* (see Luke 22:42).

3. Reverence

My covenant with him was one of life and peace, and I gave these to him; it called for reverence, and he revered me and stood in awe of my name. (Mal. 2:5)

A long time ago, there was a man who did what was right and showed great respect to God. He was not only a happy husband and father to ten wonderful children, but he was also very wealthy. He had thousands of animals, owned his own business, and had many people who worked for him. The Bible says he was the greatest man in the East.

But in one day, he lost everything: his whole business, his animals, his servants, and—worst of all—every one of his ten children. He was filled with misery!

Can you imagine how awful he must have felt? But listen to this. After hearing this devastating news, he fell to the ground and worshipped God saying, "The LORD gave and the LORD has taken away; may the name of the LORD be *praised*" (Job 1:21b NIV). Even though he was devastated, the man praised God and continued to show Him the respect and reverence He deserved. When the man was the most miserable he had ever been, he didn't say or think anything rude about God. The Bible says, "Throughout all this Job did not sin or blame God for anything" (v. 22). (See Job 1.)

Reverence is an attitude we show toward God because we recognize how great He is. This man refused to disrespect God because he knew that God was deserving of reverence.

When discussing Job's devotion to God, Satan questioned Job's motives. "Does Job *fear* God for nothing?" (v. 9). The Hebrew word for "fear" is sometimes translated as *revere*. Satan claimed that Job only feared (or revered) God because God had blessed him but said if God's blessings were taken away, Job would surely curse God. This was proven not to be true.

Job's reverence of God wasn't dependent on what God did for him. God is worthy of our reverence because of who He is, regardless of what He does. Reverence sees God as set apart, holy, mighty, all-knowing, all-powerful, all-seeing, and perfect and therefore deserving of all respect, honor, and praise. Reverence is similar to honor, only it takes things a step further. While honor is recognizing someone's greatness, reverence is fearing someone for their greatness, especially compared to our lack of it. No one can truly come before God without kneeling—whether literally or figuratively. God's character and His glory will bring us to our knees every time. That's what true reverence looks like.

Many people tend to talk to their children about reverence in the context of how to behave in church. In other words, sitting still and being quiet is considered reverent behavior. However, true reverence begins in the heart and is not limited to the church building. So while it is appropriate to speak with children about what reverence can look like in church, if we skip over what it means to have a reverent heart, I think we and our children may miss the point. I don't believe God's heart is moved by children knowing how to sit still and be quiet. I believe He is moved by reverent hearts.

 God's character and His glory will bring us to our knees every time.

Simplifying Reverence

Most children have never seen a rocket ship up close, but if they did, they would be in total amazement. We can describe the height and volume of a rocket ship, all the many people it took to build it, and what's more impressive than its mass: its power.

Rockets are powerful enough to shoot off into space! If we were to ask our children if they'd ever like to see one take off up close, they'd probably answer with an emphatic but naive "Yes!"

> While it might seem like a cool thing to be near a rocket ship when it takes off, it would actually be awful. When a rocket takes off, the flames that shoot out around it are so large that the air becomes hot enough to melt our bodies. You might want to be close to a rocket ship, but it's so powerful that standing close to it would actually be scary. People have to stand *miles* away from one when it's taking off. However, if you're inside the rocket ship, that power wouldn't hurt you at all. In fact, it would carry you high up into the sky!
>
> Did you know that God is way more powerful than a rocket ship? But one of the most beautiful things about God is that though He is powerful, He invites us to come close to Him. When we believe in God and trust Him, it's as if we get to sit inside the rocket ship and ride with Him through life!

Having reverence toward God means we recognize just how great and powerful He is. No one would ever think they were more powerful than a rocket ship, and likewise, we should never think we know better than God, can do better than God, or don't need God.

We can also teach our children how to practically revere God in many ways: by remembering that God is in control of all things, giving credit to God for all things, trusting God in all situations, speaking of Him in a way that is respectful and honoring, worshipping Him, bowing low when we pray, fasting, obeying His commands, and studying His Word.

4. Humility

Everyone who exalts himself will be humbled, and the one who humbles himself will be exalted. (Luke 14:11)

A long time ago there lived a king who did all the things that God can't stand. He was worse than any king before or after him. To make matters worse, he led the people of his kingdom away from God completely. The whole kingdom rejected God. Because of how much they opposed God, the fate of the entire country changed. Talk about a terrible king! He got what he deserved when he was taken away in shackles as a prisoner to a foreign country.

And yet, as terrible as this king was—and he was considered the worst—when he prayed, God listened to him and answered his prayer. Instead of dying in prison, the king was not only released but sent back to his homeland as king.

This king's name was Manasseh. King Manasseh was far from a model for prayer, but he did one thing right—perhaps only one thing— and that changed the course of his life. After being tied up as a prisoner, 2 Chronicles 33:12 says he *"earnestly humbled himself* before the God of his ancestors."

Perhaps he thought he could do as he pleased because he was king. But in jail, as a prisoner with no way out, he realized he was not so great after all and that God was truly his only hope. Despite all he had done to oppose, reject, and disgrace God, when he humbled himself, God granted his request. (See 2 Chron. 33:1–13.)

If there is one quality that speaks to the soft spot in God's heart more than any other, I believe it is genuine humility. Humility is the turning point of many stories in the Bible. To show us how much God values humility, He demonstrated it perfectly through His Son, who "humbled himself by becoming obedient to the point of death—even to death on a cross" (Phil. 2:8). If anyone had reason to think highly of himself, it was Jesus, yet He humbled Himself and let God lift Him up. In the same way, God promises to lift up all those who lower themselves (see James 4:10).

Humility is knowing that we are not more important than other people and especially not more important than God. Instead, we know how great God is and how insignificant we are by comparison. Humility means recognizing our deep need for God while realizing He owes us nothing. Every blessing and good thing we've been given, even our accomplishments and abilities, have been gifted to us by God. Psalms, Ecclesiastes, and James all compare humans to grass. We are susceptible to withering and fading, which means that any glory we seem to have is merely a facade. When we pray, our humility should be evident. He is God and we are not.

Simplifying Humility

Humility is an attitude we hold that recognizes God as the source of life for all things. The opposite of humility is pride, when we take our abilities and possessions for granted and fail to give God credit. When we introduce humility, we can start by helping our children see that we are utterly dependent on God. By praying with humility, we give God all the praise He deserves.

> Let me see you take a big breath.
>
> Did you know that you wouldn't be able to take a breath without God? Crazy, huh? The lungs inside your body are from God, and the air you breathe is from God. I wouldn't be able to breathe without God either. Actually, I wouldn't be able to do anything without God. If it weren't for God's great love for us, we wouldn't even be alive!
>
> Everything we are, everything we have, everything we can do is all because of God. We practice humility when we remember that we can't do *anything* without God and *everything* we have is from Him.

5. Fasting

> I turned my attention to the Lord God to seek him by prayer and petitions, with fasting, sackcloth, and ashes. (Dan. 9:3)

The king of Judah was shocked when he received news that several neighboring nations were banding together to attack his country. Not only had his enemies joined together, they were already on their way! The king became nervous and afraid. Rather than send word for all the soldiers to assemble, he told everyone to pray to God for help and join him in fasting. The whole country united with the king in praying and fasting.

God answered their prayers for help. He told them they wouldn't have to fight their enemies. Instead of sending soldiers out, the king sent the worship leaders out! And guess what. God made the enemies fight each other. The people of Judah never even had to lift their swords. (See 2 Chron. 20:1–23.)

To show how much we need God, we can fast, or take a break from eating food. Sometimes people fast on a special occasion or for a special reason, as this king did. Other times, people regularly fast as a reminder that they need God.

Food has been an expression of how we feel for centuries. Various cultures throughout time have celebrated with food. Our culture is no exception, with food generally taking center stage at weddings, holidays, and all kinds of gatherings. However, our culture differs from biblical times in how we respond to sadness, sorrow, or dire times. While we might binge Netflix and pizza when we're feeling terrible, Jewish people in the Bible practiced something very different: self-denial. People typically showed self-denial by tearing their clothes, wearing uncomfortable clothes (sackcloth), putting ashes on their heads, and abstaining from food. Though fasting is often associated with food, denying ourselves a specific kind of comfort or pleasure for a time can accomplish the same thing.

Sometimes our obsession with food and satiation inhibits our ability to be earnest in prayer. Doesn't it make sense that when there's reason to celebrate, we feast, but when things are dire, we fast? Fasting sobers up our hearts and souls from all our self-indulgence and pleasure seeking. It helps us focus our prayers and dependence on God. It's a physical representation of our spiritual resolve to seek and depend on God.

Fasting is also the ultimate form of humility; hence, Jesus instructed us not to brag about fasting. He said, essentially, to take a shower, dress normally, and look nice when you're fasting. Don't be puffed up, or it will ruin the point of your fasting.

Simplifying Fasting

To help our children grasp the value of fasting, we can start by explaining that when something is important to us, we usually give up other things.

Remember that art project you did last month? You wanted it to be really good, but that meant you had to give up a few things in order to work on it. You didn't watch the family movie that week, and you stayed up extra late to finish it. You gave up a movie and sleep in order to work on the art project because it was more important to you.

Sometimes we give up other things in order to talk to God with more focus and seriousness.

Choosing not to eat food is called fasting, but people practice fasting in other ways too, like by not doing certain activities or by giving up TV or game time, entertainment, dessert, or candy. We can even fast together as a family.

I have talked to my children about fasting and left it up to them. Two of the five have practiced skipping meals intentionally, for a specific time and reason, but not until age eight or so. Here are some healthy boundaries to help us confidently introduce fasting to our children:

- Be sure your child understands the role and purpose of fasting.
- Make sure you and they have a clear reason for fasting.
- Work together to decide on a reasonable time frame.

- Discuss what fasting will look like (a skipped meal, no dinner, no TV, etc.).

Faith, persistence, reverence, humility, and fasting are some of the many excellent heart qualities we can encourage in our children from an early age to grow their prayer lives. But don't stop there! As you read through the Bible on your own, keep an eye out for more. Modeling and nurturing the qualities we see in the lives of these bold men and women will help point our children's hearts in the right direction and, over time, bring them closer to God in prayer.

Chapter 9

THE GOLDEN HOUR

Praying and Ministering One on One

It's not hard for my second-grade son to get frustrated. His ideal day consists of nothing but play … so he's often disappointed. After a few days of him seeming particularly frustrated, I pulled him aside so we could talk. "I've noticed you've been really frustrated lately. Do you know why that is?" He explained all the different things that had been upsetting him the previous couple of days. A comment his sister made, the way a game ended—all things I saw happen and understood. So I prodded a little more. "Hmm, do you feel frustrated about these things all the time? Do they bother you even when they're over?" After a little chatting, he went on to explain one event in particular.

As I listened, I realized that underneath the frustrations of these recent days lay the nagging memory of an interaction he'd had with another child months ago. Because the situation was never resolved, it kept the pressure inside him high, depleting his capacity to handle new irritating situations.

We talked about it for a while. I explained why he logically should not be so bothered by this anymore. However, even as I was offering "solutions," I could tell they were not changing his mind or feelings. He still carried weight and pain. So we decided to pray about it. My experience has taught me that this is exactly the kind of thing that Jesus loves to heal.

In my heart, I turned to God for help and guidance. Then I said, "How do you think Jesus feels about what happened? Do you think He understands your sadness and frustration?" Josiah thought about it a minute and concluded that, yes, Jesus definitely understood. I then explained to him that sometimes we are burdened by things we don't need to be burdened by and we can ask Jesus to take those burdens away.

"Buddy, sit next to me. Close your eyes, and imagine taking that memory and handing it to Jesus. He is happy to take it from you. Now every time you start to think about it, remember that you gave that thought and that burden to Jesus. Just like He takes our sins away, He can take away our burdens too."

We then prayed and asked Jesus to take the burden from Josiah and help him to not feel its weight anymore but to remember that Jesus carries our burdens. Josiah felt markedly better after that. It was obvious he was no longer carrying the same weight. I circled back around to him several days later, and he confirmed the event hadn't come up in his mind at all. He still has a tendency to get frustrated. Because disappointment can pile up inside him easily, I learned through this initial experience and subsequent ones that he regularly needs to pray through things so he doesn't carry the weight of them around.

Prior to that conversation, I was beginning to get irritated with his behavior, not realizing something deeper was going on. I'm so glad we sat down together. If I hadn't taken the time to sit and talk with him, I might never have realized how much he was hurting.

What about your children? What kinds of things do they struggle with? Sometimes it takes sitting one on one with our children to help them sort out their thoughts and feelings. But more importantly, through those conversations, we can guide them into the regular practice of seeking God in prayer.

The Dance

So far, we've been taking our children by the hand, and they've been getting little tastes of God's presence as we've prayed together. They've been learning how to engage God with honest hearts and all kinds of other good things, but this is where things begin to shift. Remember: our ultimate hope is for our children to seek Jesus *on their own*.

You know that dance move where you spin your partner in close to you? You turn them right up your arm and into your chest. Do you remember what happens next? After bringing them in close, you twirl them out and let go so they can keep spinning on their own. These next two chapters are going to be like that dance move. In this chapter we're going to bring our children in real close for one-on-one prayer. Then, in the next chapter, we're going to spin them out and let go so they can keep praying, on their own.

One-on-One Prayer

While I've written mostly in terms of praying with multiple children or as a family, hopefully you've realized that most, if not all, of these techniques and ideas can be adopted for use with just one child. In fact, my experience has been that no matter what technique or approach I take in prayer, when I'm alone with just one child, it's always more meaningful. Up until now we have not specifically addressed the beauty and necessity of praying one on one with our children.

Remember my friend I told you about early on who has children with various special needs? After she finally gave up on her ideal scenario for prayer and family devotions, she discovered that her children responded great to one-on-one times of prayer. Alone with just one child, she and/or her husband can sit to listen, talk, and pray with them at the level they will individually understand.

While praying together as a family is hugely important, it is not the same as praying with just one child. It's during these special times, whether we're on the couch together or sitting on the edge of their bed, that we are able to give them our full attention, listen to their concerns, and pray with them. These are also ideal times to explain the good news of Jesus!

Think about your son or daughter. Where are they at in life right now? What kinds of things might you talk and pray about when you sit down, just the two of you? And when is an ideal time to be alone with this one child?

For most parents, the best time to pray with one child is before bed. Most (but not all) of the bedtime routine functions as an on-ramp, bringing your child to the place where they are lying in bed and (hopefully) calm.

Once my children are all cozy, I love to begin by recounting the day's events: things that were fun, difficult, hurtful, all of it. At some point, I realized I not only wanted my children to remember a lot about their childhood (hence, reviewing their day before bed), but I also didn't want them going to bed angry, bitter, hurt, and the like, especially if a simple conversation would help relieve their stress.

Whenever possible, view these one-on-one times as opportunities to ask questions, and let your child talk as much as they want. Maybe they're having trouble with a friend or feeling stressed or confused about something at school. Or perhaps they've been brainstorming their latest hopes and dreams and would *love* to tell you all about it. Likely, what you end up praying about will come out of your conversation together.

Here are some questions that have the potential to lead you both into a time of prayer:

- Did anything from today upset you?
- Are you looking forward to tomorrow?
- Is there anything you want to pray about before bed?
- Is there anyone you need to forgive before you go to sleep?
- What do you want to thank God for before you fall asleep?
- Who do you want to pray for before bed tonight?
- Who do you think we should pray for tonight? Let's close our eyes a moment and see if there's anyone God brings to mind for us to pray for.

Praying with Littles

For a few years, my husband worked at UPS, loading trucks at an ungodly hour each morning. During that season, I would get up early to read and pray before the day started. I was pregnant with my third child, and my second oldest typically slept in, but my oldest was an early riser. Thankfully, many mornings she was content to sit with me on the bed while I read and prayed.

While I had intended those early hours to be a time to pray alone, they turned into a special time when my oldest and I read together, prayed together, and talked about the Bible for a long time. It was a short season because the dynamics changed just a few months later. My third daughter was born and my oldest started school, so this morning time became impossible.

It sounds rather idyllic when I describe my oldest snuggling in bed for prayer. But if I'm being completely honest, it wasn't at first. It was kind of annoying that she woke up so early. After all, I was only up so I could read and pray *by myself.* Thankfully, though I didn't see it at first, I was able to embrace that time. And I'm so glad I did.

While in the process of moving last year, I came across a small notebook with big spirals. It looked as if it had been tossed off the bunk bed one too many times, and the pages were bent, folded, and half-ripped. As I flipped through it, I realized it was my daughter's prayer journal from when she was very little. Many of the drawings I had shown her on paper she redrew on her own in her journal.

During these dedicated prayer times, our children's connection to God grows deeper, like the roots of the tree in Jeremiah 17 that grow toward the stream. These moments may not feel glorious and we may have one hundred other things on our to-do lists, but praying with our children is special. I had no idea that the mornings we spent together were also impacting her alone times of prayer.

When Our Children Are Hurting

Inevitably, you'll encounter a situation where you realize your child is really hurting. Maybe they've been angry and rude to everyone all morning or they've been more withdrawn than usual. Whatever the outward symptom, it's likely there's another problem at the root. Sometimes the issue is rather simple: they need individual positive attention, or they're hungry or tired. But sometimes when you're alone with them in a calm environment, you'll discover there is a deeper hurt.

If they are in a place to receive it, you can talk it through with them and then pray together. When we pray with someone for any type of healing, whether inner or physical, we are ministering to that person through prayer with faith that Jesus will bring healing, comfort, wholeness, peace ... whatever it is they need. We can minister to our children in this way as well.

In the situation with my son that I mentioned at the beginning of this chapter, it was through the course of our conversation that I realized there was a deeper problem and that he needed some inner healing and comfort. After he took a moment to realize that Jesus understood his frustration, it was a natural next step to trust Him with that situation completely. By the time we prayed, my son was ready, and we knew what specifically we were asking Jesus to do. Let's take a closer look at the steps I walked through with my son.

Steps for Ministering to Children

There are a variety of approaches people take when it comes to prayer ministry. I've created five basic steps for ministering to children based on what I've learned from various ministries, my own experience, and Scripture.

1. Gather information.

Ask questions and listen carefully as your child talks. I listened as my son vented his frustration about many recent events that was building up inside him. While listening to him, I was also listening for insight from the Holy Spirit. I prayed, *Jesus, show me what's going on here.*

2. Find the root cause or an original event.

Ask gently probing questions to see if there's an event where everything seemed to start or a deeper root cause. In other words, you want to find what is at the core of this problem. When talking with my son, I didn't even know there was an original event. Thankfully, because I asked a few questions about his frustration and the timing of it all, I discovered there was.

Sometimes a root cause isn't an actual event but a lie or misunderstanding that has led to a whole host of issues. For instance, in trying to find out why your daughter is fighting with her sister, you may discover that there's a root of jealousy, resentment, unforgiveness, or bitterness.

3. Look at Jesus.

When Jesus healed, He wasn't only demonstrating His authority over sickness, demons, and death. He was also demonstrating something remarkable about His character. Over and over, we're shown that Jesus healed out of *love and compassion*. It's our tendency to approach prayer with our hands out, but nothing that Jesus may place in our hands could be greater than knowing Him and the depths of His love. If our children receive healing from Jesus but miss His love, they'll be no better off.

I asked my son, "How do you think Jesus feels about what happened? Do you think He understands your sadness and frustration?" Before praying, ask your child to pause and "look" at Jesus. What does Jesus say about this? How does He feel about the situation? Any time we engage Jesus, it is to learn more about Him and His character, not just to receive from Him.

 Nothing that Jesus may place in our hands could be greater than knowing Him and the depths of His love.

4. Address everything in prayer with Jesus.

Take a moment or two to pause and posture your own heart before praying. Next, I find it helpful to think of prayer time as making an exchange with Jesus. We give Him our _____ (brokenness, pain, hurt, jealousy, anger, etc.) and ask Him to give us His _____ (wholeness, peace, healing, thankfulness, joy, etc.). It often helps to be as specific in our requests as possible. Close with you or your child asking Jesus to fill you both with His Holy Spirit.

5. Follow up.

Finally, ask your child how they feel. Do they feel better or worse, at peace or confused? If need be, pray a second or third time. Be sure to tell your child that you will continue to pray for them on your own too. And make sure you do! Just because they feel better doesn't necessarily mean you won't have to pray about that issue again later. Similarly, if they seem to be no better, you might spend some more time talking about it, but it's okay to pray with them about it again at another time; it doesn't have to happen right then. In fact, a little space will allow you time to talk with God and ask Him for more wisdom and discernment.

A Few Things to Note

Ministering to our children through prayer can be incredibly powerful and meaningful, but there are a couple of things we need to note.

Though ministering to our children can be very effective, our children may still benefit from talking and praying with a youth leader, pastor, counselor, or someone else. While we as parents have a lot of love to give, that doesn't mean we are equipped to handle every situation that comes along. And for some things, our children may have an easier time talking with someone other than us. Similarly, our children may need medical help or professional counseling. If you feel your child may benefit from counseling services or medical intervention, this doesn't mean that God won't, can't, or hasn't brought about healing. Perhaps He will bring it about in a different way.

Second, use lots of caution when ministering to your children through prayer if the present state of your relationship with them is not in a good place. Perhaps the problems they're having are because what they really need is to mend things with you. It might cause more damage if we try to bring healing in one area when we've neglected to do the work to fix our broken relationship first. This may be a perfect opportunity to tag team with your spouse or other trusted adult.

Additionally, while it is often helpful to ask probing questions to gather information, we should be sensitive to the fact that when our children share, they may end up feeling exposed and vulnerable. While we all hope our children will feel comfortable telling us anything and everything, we should be aware of cues that they may not be ready to share.

 We should keep in mind that our goal is not to uncover every deep and hidden secret but rather to help our children heal by bringing them to Jesus.

While our hope is that our time with them will help them grow closer to God, this won't be the case if they feel uncomfortable. The Bible shares story after story of God protecting people from shame and disgrace, rather than exposing them. We should keep in mind that our goal is not to uncover every deep and hidden secret but rather to help our children heal by bringing them to Jesus.

Last, praying with our children is not a one-time event. There's no need to rush or push. We'll have many chances to pray with them about many things. If you sense there is more going on that your child is not sharing or feel there's more that needs help or healing, reassure them that you will continue to pray for them and that you are available to talk more at any time. Sometimes our children go through hard and difficult seasons. If your child is resistant to all your efforts, hang tight; we're going to tackle that in chapter 11.

A Note about Physical Healing

Though this doesn't exclusively apply to one-on-one prayer, now is the best time to discuss physical healing. On a few occasions I've felt prompted by the Holy Spirit to command healing rather than request it. It was as if the Holy Spirit within me was ready to move and I was just the vessel delivering His desire. This approach seems to be the norm in accounts of healing in Scripture. Perhaps you remember Peter and John saying to the lame man, "In the name of Jesus Christ of Nazareth, get up and walk!" (Acts 3:6b). And imagine the shock for people present when Jesus' booming voice cut through the crowd of mourners with the command, "Lazarus, come out!" (John 11:43).

On one occasion, I had been up with my daughter all night. She was probably only six or so, and she had a stomach bug. The worst part for her was not the throwing up but all the time in between. She'd hold on to the toilet bowl and cry over it, knowing that her body was going to vomit again but not knowing when. It was a dreadful feeling for her. She could not rest or get comfortable, let alone doze off.

I tried to comfort her the best I could, but I was exhausted and barely able to keep my eyes open. For hours, I continued to pray with every conscious thought I had as she continued to throw up. Finally, after the poor thing had been crying for who knows how long, I felt something well up inside me. I sat up, gave her a firm pat on the back as I declared, "Do it, Lord!" The moment my hand made contact with her back, she threw up *a lot*. And that was the end. Within minutes, she fell asleep and slept soundly the rest of the night. After agonizing for hours, it was finally over.

It was as though all my travailing prayers overflowed into that moment when God finally acted. Somehow I knew I needed to whack (gently, of course) her back and that would be the end. And it was.

On another occasion, my son, who was not even one, was suffering from anaphylactic shock, though we didn't realize it at the time. We called the ambulance when his lips started to turn blue, but before the paramedics got there, he became incredibly lethargic. He got to the point where he didn't even respond to our desperate voices calling out his name. It felt like we were losing him in our arms.

Finally, my husband, full of authority, put his hand on Malachi and declared, "Be healed in Jesus' name." At that moment, Malachi lifted his head and turned to see Grandpa Tom walk in the door. Waking from his lethargy, he reached out for him as he usually did. By the time the EMTs arrived, he looked so good I had to defend myself: "I swear, just moments ago I thought we were going to lose him!"

It's not my husband's nature or personality to *command* healing. I know some people pray like that regularly, and I find nothing wrong with that approach. We see that type of prayer frequently throughout the Old and New Testaments. However, in that moment, I believe the command my husband gave came from the Holy Spirit within him.

I share these stories not so you'll begin slapping your children's backs and yelling, "Do it, Lord!" Please don't. But rather, I share them to encourage you to listen to the promptings of the Holy Spirit while you pray. At times it may be appropriate to command healing. My experience has been, and we know from Scripture, that this is a work of the Holy Spirit, not something we can conjure up or try to make happen on our own terms.

I'm so excited for the times of prayer you're going to have with your children! I believe those moments are going to be incredibly meaningful and fruitful. Now, all this discussion about praying with one child was the "spin in" part of the dance. Next, we're going to work on the "spin out" to see how we can help our children pray on their own.

LETTING GO

Helping Them Pray on Their Own

"Lord, change me!" I wrote these desperate words in my spiral-bound journal as a teen while in one of my favorite places: my bedroom. I loved that bedroom because it was full of all my favorite things: Simpsons posters pinned to my lime-green walls, a tie-dyed tapestry that hung from the ceiling above my bed, a string of purple star lights decorating my mirror, a green Volkswagen beetle lamp, and of course, pictures of my friends and me everywhere. My room felt like the perfect representation of all the things I loved.

Looking back, my room was a lot more than colors and decor that represented my likes. My bedroom was the place I could be alone. It was the place I could think without other distractions or opinions. It was within those lime-green walls that I poured my heart out to God with raw honesty. It was under that tie-dyed sheet that I wrestled through some of my hardest times.

It was alone in my bedroom at age eight that I spoke with God so tenderly and genuinely to receive Jesus for the first time. In fact, as I think through all my bedrooms, from childhood to now, I find that each of them hosted countless meetings with God. They represented precious encounters with Jesus. It's no wonder He said, "When you pray, go into your room and shut the door" (Matt. 6:6a ESV).

We can only take our children so far. The intimacy we desire for them to experience in prayer is unlikely to happen with us right there. While we can do an excellent job teaching them to pray and bringing them to Jesus on all sorts of occasions, our ultimate hope needs to be for them to seek Him, know Him, and commune with Him *on their own.*

The Biblical Practice of Getting Alone to Pray

We don't know if David was alone when he wrote many of the psalms, but it certainly seems like he was. Many of them contain a level of intimacy and honesty that give the impression it was just him and God and he was laying it all out for the Lord. The full range of emotion and vulnerability that David expressed to God would not likely be seen by a king in public. (Then again, David did some other strange things in public, so who knows?)

David understood something that I often miss: no place on earth compares to being in God's presence. As king, he could have traveled many places and spent his time in plenty of other locations, but he said,

> I have asked one thing from the LORD;
> it is what I desire:
> to dwell in the house of the LORD
> all the days of my life,

gazing on the beauty of the LORD
and seeking him in his temple. (Ps. 27:4)

David got it. He was so mesmerized by God's magnificence that he couldn't think of anything he'd rather do than seek Him.

Whether it was David in the house of God, Moses on top of Mount Sinai, Hannah in the temple, Daniel kneeling in his upper room, or Jesus praying in the garden, we see story after story of men and women who knew the value of separating themselves from other people and activities to meet with God. There's something about being alone with God that allows for deeper intimacy, vulnerability, and clarity.

Getting alone in prayer, whether in a room or on the side of a mountain, is a foundational practice for Christ followers. Let's pause here for just a moment. Raise your hand if you'd describe your personal times of prayer as "gazing on the beauty of the LORD." You in the back? Oh no, they were just stretching. Unfortunately, the majority of us would not describe our prayer times this way. For many of us, just staying awake is a challenge.

 There's something about being alone with God that allows for deeper intimacy, vulnerability, and clarity.

So how can we give our children *quality* prayer times? How can we ensure that prayer for them is like it was for David? Well, we can't. We can't ensure they'll be captivated by God's glory, nor should we try to, because that's God's job, not ours. However, what we *can* do is set them up well—we can take them by the hand (at first) by providing good instruction, and we can provide some helpful resources.

Offer a Doable Plan

We've already discussed that while there is no formula for prayer, it can sometimes help to have a plan. Likewise, quiet times don't need to be formulaic, but it can help to give our children a plan to guide their time so when they show up, they don't get stuck thinking, *What now?*

The acronym PRAY can easily be used to guide our personal prayers, but if you want to introduce your children to a plan that includes Bible reading, here's a simple one:

> **Read Scripture.** Some families read the Bible together, some assign a book or reading plan, and some let their children read a psalm or whatever they feel like from a book of the Bible. Any of these will work.

> **Write Scripture.** Show your child that when they read the Bible, they might come across a story or a verse they really like. If so, they should write it down in their journal. That way, later, they can come back and be encouraged by some passages/stories. You might even encourage them to pay

attention to verses that teach them something about God and what He is like or Scriptures that would make good prayers.

Intercede. Your child can then spend some time praying for themself and others. We're going to talk more about this shortly.

Journal. This is an opportunity for your child to write out thoughts or prayers in a casual way. They can talk to God and pause to let Him talk back. Younger children may prefer to draw instead of write, or they may not want to do either. That's all fine. The point is simply to talk with God.

Very young children will not be ready to do this on their own, but we can practice this (or a simplified version) with them until they are. Don't feel like they need to attempt all the steps every time. Sometimes they may only do one or a combination.

Provide Good Resources: Bibles and Journals

How many times have you heard a friend say that she's doing a new study that she *just loves*? Naturally, you reply, "Oh, cool! What's the study?" If you're anything like me, that information gets filed in the back of your mind and lost forever. Just like your friend who's been having success with a new resource, our children can benefit from good resources.

In my experience, all our children really need is an age-appropriate Bible and a journal. My husband and I like to buy some kind of Bible or study book for our kids each Easter (though you could pick any holiday). We have found Christianbook.com to be a useful site. You'll find an endless number of books, Bibles, studies, devotionals, and more there.

When looking for a Bible, find one that will work well for your child's age and reading ability. A simple storybook Bible with lots of pictures and simple text may be perfect for early readers and children who don't read yet. The New International Readers Version is a simplified edition of the New International Version that's specifically meant for early readers. *The Action Bible* is fun for children who can read, as well as for those who are highly visual. There are also several different types of study Bibles meant for children who are in elementary or middle school.

I gave my life to Christ at eight years old because of an invitation I read in my Precious Moments storybook Bible. I was old enough to read something more advanced, but this version was much easier. If you're debating between two different options, go for the simpler one.

The next best resource is a journal. I try to make sure my children always have a journal they can write and draw in. If one of them says they don't have a journal, meaning they've used one all up, they might as well be saying, "We're out of milk!" And I'll get them a journal the next chance I get.

Most of my children have a Bible, a journal, and maybe a few other reading or drawing materials in a bin under or beside their beds. When they go to sleep at night, it's all right there for them to pull out and use.

Now, if you're reading this thinking, *I don't know if my six-year-old boy is a journal person*, I get it. I have several of those! Not six-year-old boys but kids who don't care for journaling. But bear with me for a minute. Even if they only use it a few times a year, it's still worth it. They will still be connecting with God through it and recording verses or memories in it.

I used to just give everyone an empty notebook with lined paper, until I realized I could help their prayer times significantly by dividing their journal into three different sections. In fact, my one daughter who historically didn't care for journaling at all took quite a liking to it when I made a couple of changes. After you set their journals up for them the first time, older kids will be able to do it by themselves.

Setting Up Your Child's Journal

The following suggestions are geared toward school-age children, but I have included modifications at the end of this section that specifically address our very young ones.

First, when picking out a journal, look for a notebook that is about half the size of a piece of paper, give or take. I prefer spirals or a binding that lays truly flat. Also, choose one with lines that are appropriately spaced for your child (college or wide ruled).

Open to one of the first pages, and write a brief message to create a dedication page. For example:

This is for Lilly. I pray that you will fill this journal
with all kinds of thoughts and prayers, dreams
and goals, struggles and successes. I pray it is a
place for you to meet with your Father in heaven,
who loves you dearly.

In the middle of the next page write "VERSES" in large letters. Then dog-ear the top and bottom of the page, creating a
type of divider. This will be the first section. The next ten pages
or so are to be used for writing verses or passages that stand out
to them. Any time they read the Bible and come across a good
verse, or their pastor or youth leader mentions a verse they want
to remember, they can write it down in this section. These pages
can be flipped back to any time. In fact, sometimes they might not
do anything else in their quiet time but reread some meaningful
verses.

The next section is reserved for intercession. Write
"INTERCESSION" in big letters, and dog-ear the top and bottom of the page. Leave the next ten pages or so for this section.
Here your child will write, draw, or make different lists of things
to pray for and about. These pages can be referred to over and
over again when praying. We're going to come back to this section in just a minute and talk about helping our children develop
the habit of interceding.

Last, title the next section "JOURNAL," and fold the top and
bottom of the page as before. The whole rest of the notebook is to be
used as any journal would be. Sometimes they'll chronicle events

from the day; other times they will be praying and wrestling with God. Older ones will likely write, while younger ones may fill these pages with drawings, doodles, or even random scribbles. All these creative outlets work as they each represent time spent with God.

Hopefully you noticed that the way we just set up the journal corresponds perfectly with the quiet time routine I suggested: read Scripture, write verses, intercede, and journal.

Setting Up the Intercession Section of the Journal

Let's go back to the intercession section for a moment. When you read what I'm about to suggest, you may have the same feeling I have when I think we're almost done with our homeschooling for the day and I read in our lesson that we still need to conduct an involved experiment. *Ugh! Do we have to do that?* No, you don't. However, if you do, I'm convinced it will help your children truly step into their calling as Christians by understanding and developing the practice of interceding for God's work to be done here on earth.

As we discussed earlier, all prayers of intercession are an extension of Jesus' prayer, "Your kingdom come. Your will be done on earth as it is in heaven" (Matt. 6:10). We want our children to have a deep personal relationship with Christ; at the same time, we are raising them to look beyond themselves and be active members of the body of Christ who are used by God in powerful ways. So let's discuss how we can expand their prayer requests beyond themselves and the things that affect only them.

When we teach our children to pray, they often have no trouble praying for themselves. And they typically have an easy time praying for the people very close to them, like Mom, Dad, and siblings. But the less connected a person is to our children's lives, the harder it will be for our kids to pray for them. Take praying for the governor, for instance. The governor is so far removed from our children's daily world that they're going to have a hard time praying for him or her.

To have them practice and grow in their ability to intercede, we're going to have our children start by praying for themselves but then gradually move further and further out to things and people that are of virtually no interest to them.

Picture concentric circles. These circles represent your child's world. The smallest center ring is your child. The ring just outside your child is the next closest thing to them: family. The ring outside that one is the next most important area. Maybe friends or relatives. The next ring represents school, their sports team, perhaps church, and so on. The farther out you travel from the center, the less "important" the categories are to your child. The last ring or two would be things like your state, your country, and possibly the world. Though we could break our children's world into dozens of concentric circles, let's limit it to five or six.

Before we continue, go ahead and fill out the categories here or on a separate piece of paper for your child. If you have multiple children, complete this exercise for just one child for now. You can go back and do this for each of the others later.

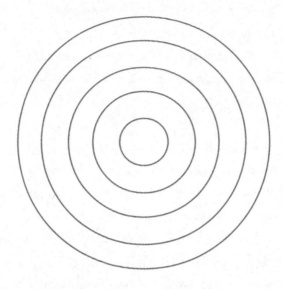

Once we've broken down our children's world into progressively expanding categories, the next step is to write each category at the top of a different page in the intercession section of their journal. The top of the first page of the section might be labeled "Prayers for Myself." The second page might read "Prayers for My Family," and so on.

Last, sit down with your child and together start making lists of what you could pray about for each category. This could take a little time, so there's no need to do them all at once, and the lists don't need to be extensive—just a few items to get them started. Here's an example list of what your child might pray in the church category:

- for everyone to be filled with the Holy Spirit
- for the pastor to give wisdom

- for the pastor's family to be protected
- for the leadership to be wise
- for the families of the church to be healthy
- for the congregation to love God with all their hearts

Imagine your child praying from this list regularly or every day if they want to. When you sit down together, just give them little prompts and let them think of as much as possible. If they don't like to write, you can write for them. We can get our children into the habit of praying now for things that will greatly impact the rest of their lives, like marrying a godly person, attending the right school or college, having good friends, being healthy, and so on.

If you think it might help, you could go one step further and assign a day of the week to each category. For instance:

Sunday: myself
Monday: my family
Tuesday: my friends
Wednesday: my sports team and school
Thursday: my church (families, leaders, etc.)
Friday: the world (including missionaries)

This way, if they're not sure what to pray about, they can just flip to the day of the week and start praying from that list.

These intercession lists are intended to be prayed from repeatedly and with relative ease. This is a good opportunity to remind our children that praying from lists helps us pray *persistently* (like the widow we learned about in chapter 8.) As your child begins using the lists, remind them that they can add to them when they think of more. If they're having trouble with a friend at school, for example, mention that they can add that issue to the list about friends. Or maybe you read an article about something that happened in another state or country. That issue could be added to the list for the state or world.

 We can get our children into the habit of praying now for things that will greatly impact the rest of their lives.

Journal Modifications

Very young and beginning readers are going to have more success if we hold their hand through the process and continue to pray with them. It's also perfectly okay to keep everything simple.

Depending on the age and personality of your child, you'll want to make some adjustments to how you set up their journal. For instance, if your child is young, consider the stick figure drawing we discussed in chapter 7. It may work well to have a simple drawing of your home, complete with little stick figure family members on one page. Other pages may contain your church building, their friends, their school, and so on. Once we draw those pictures in their journal, they can flip to that page whenever they want and use it to inspire their prayers.

For children under five, consider keeping prayers focused on those within the four walls of your home. Draw each family member on a different page—maybe even the family pet. When you feel they're ready, gradually add others who are close to them, such as grandparents, friends, and teachers.

Make adjustments and modifications to fit your child, and be creative! Each child will be different, and there's no need to force any certain outcomes. While my oldest daughter was drawing out prayers in her journal at three, my five-year-old son wants nothing to do with his journal. Some of that could be due to the fact that I've put in significantly less effort with him, especially compared with my oldest, but it's also indicative of his personality and interests.

As your children grow and change, so can their journals. My other daughter who didn't use her journal for a long time took a big liking to the "Verses" section, which she uses almost exclusively. In her next journal, that section will probably be the largest.

Hopefully, time spent alone with God in a journal will be as meaningful to your child as it was for me growing up. But keep two things in mind. One, their journal is just a tool—an effective tool in my opinion, but still just a tool. If we push it too much, it will become a burden. Two, part of what made my time with God so meaningful growing up was that I pursued Him on my own. We can set our children up well, but then we need to step back. This is about giving them the opportunity to seek God out of their own desire.

We've covered a lot regarding prayer, but sometimes, despite our best intentions and all the preparation, things don't go as we hope. In fact, you may have been reading along and thought, *I can't do any of this. You don't know what we've been through or how difficult my child can be.* I get it. Sometimes we go through seasons that stretch us beyond what we feel we can handle. In this next chapter, we're going to look at the role of prayer with our kids when we're in the middle of a really hard time.

Chapter 11

PRAYING IN
HARD TIMES

Trials, Resistant Children, and Spiritual Warfare

A friend of mine struggled to raise her three children while living with a suicidal and abusive husband for twelve of their thirty years of marriage. She said, "People don't believe me when I say I had to reach down and pick up my right knee to make myself take a step. Then I had to pick up my left one and take another step." The amount of shock and trauma she experienced was paralyzing. "To me, prayer was life. Prayer put breath in my lungs. If it weren't for prayer, I wouldn't be alive. There were times I couldn't even take a breath and I just prayed, 'God, fill my lungs with air.' And He did!"

In seasons of trauma and tragedy, prayer is our breath. When it feels like there is nothing else to sustain us, God will. In these times, don't worry about details such as your approach or whether you're being creative. Just talk to God. Just pray and pray and pray some more. Keep breathing. Our children will watch us pray, and they will see us lean into the hands of God to cry and wrestle, sometimes feeling like we can't breathe. But allowing our children to see us live in the palms of our Creator's hands is the best thing we could possibly model for them.

Life doesn't always go how we hope or plan. In fact, life often brings us things we're not prepared for and don't feel equipped to handle. If you're in the middle of a hard season, my heart goes out to you. I pray that God will wrap His arms of love and comfort around you. I pray that you will continue to use prayer as your breath to get through each day.

If you're not in a hard season, I encourage you to read this chapter anyway. The reality is, we all go through storms of some kind. Think of this chapter as preparation. Learning how to navigate and prioritize in hard times now will help tremendously when those storms inevitably come.

 In seasons of trauma and tragedy, prayer is our breath.

Lean into God

As much as I wish it weren't the case, I often refuse to be comforted when I'm in pain. Maybe you've experienced this before too. You push away the very people who are trying to help—your spouse, parents, or a friend.

Sometimes we resist comfort and choose to sit in pain because allowing ourselves to be comforted can feel like moving on and we're simply not ready to do that. Other times we resist comfort because we don't feel anyone can understand or fix the depths of our pain. "Thanks for the offer, but no, a hug isn't going to fix this gaping wound."

If you're feeling like you want to push everyone away and never let them in again, that's normal. It's a natural response to put protective walls around our hearts when we're hurting. We do this instinctively to protect ourselves from further pain. The key to healing is to put up walls that are intentional, not knee-jerk reactions to our pain. Let me explain the difference.

Intentional walls, or boundaries, provide us with the protection we need for healing to occur. Setting up boundaries allows us freedom to soften our hearts to God and let Him work in us. When we put up walls as a knee-jerk reaction to our pain, though, our hearts become places where pain and bitterness fester. Many people equate putting up walls with being hard-hearted. But becoming hard-hearted happens when we not only resist comfort and keep others at a distance but also keep God at a distance and choose to sit in a type of prideful pain.

As I look back at my hardest seasons and most painful memories, I needed those boundaries to protect myself and provide myself with time and space to process. To be fair, I almost always let my husband inside those walls because God has blessed me with an understanding and tenderhearted man. For you, that person may be your spouse or a good friend. But you might also do most of your processing alone with God. Like a full-term mother cat that's waited until all the children of the house are asleep and tucked away in their beds before crawling into a dark and hidden space to focus on labor, when we're alone with God, away from others' thoughts and opinions, we're safe to be vulnerable and tender and to express all our pain just as it is.

It is from this intimate place that we'll see just how right the psalmist was when he said: "The LORD is close to the broken-hearted and saves those who are crushed in spirit" (Ps. 34:18 NIV).

Why am I taking the time to talk about the importance of leaning into God in challenging seasons? Isn't this book about praying with children? Well, yes, and that's exactly why it's important. Not only do we need to receive from God for our own health, grieving, and healing, but we also need to be connected to the Source of life in order to minister to our children.

After Paul names God the "God of all comfort," he says, "He comforts us in all our affliction, *so that we may be able to comfort* those who are in any kind of affliction, through the comfort we ourselves receive from God" (2 Cor. 1:3–4). He comforts us so that we can then comfort others.

A friend of mine experienced a family death not long ago. When talking about what life looked like for them in that season, she stressed the importance of her and her husband using the evenings to do their own processing with God and each other so they could be available for their children during the day. Her example does not mean we can fix everything for our children or take away their pain. But if we spend time receiving love from God, then even if we are weak and hurting, we will still be able to be present and available for our children.

Spiritual Warfare

There may be times, maybe even long seasons, that we feel off or unsettled, and we might even wonder, *Is our family under some kind of attack?*

There is a lot we don't know about the spiritual realm or how Satan and his fallen angels operate. But we do know that our prayers affect spiritual activity (see Dan. 10), and we are also told how to stand firm and battle.

Consider the following passage from Ephesians:

> Be strengthened by the Lord and by his vast strength. Put on the full armor of God so that you can stand against the schemes of the devil. For our struggle is not against flesh and blood, but against the rulers, against the authorities, against the cosmic powers of this darkness, against evil, spiritual forces in the heavens.…
>
> Take the helmet of salvation and the sword of the Spirit—which is the word of God. Pray at all times in the Spirit with every prayer and request, and stay alert with all perseverance and intercession for all the saints. (6:10–12, 17–18)

Though entire books have been written on this passage about preparing ourselves for spiritual battle, we're going look at four practical takeaways.

1. Know Your Enemy

The first thing to note from this passage is that our battle is not against each other. When there is stress in the house, the easiest thing to do is to attack the people there with us. Instead, we should recognize the true Enemy and use prayer as our weapon against him.

2. Use Scripture

After Jesus fasted for forty days and forty nights, He was feeling weak. It's no surprise that's exactly the time Satan came to tempt Him. Every time Satan tried to launch an attack, Jesus blocked it. He resisted Satan three times. He didn't speak theology, give a three-point sermon, or pray anything dramatic. He simply quoted Scripture. Then Satan left.

We can use Scripture like a sword to fight against the Enemy. We can pray Scripture, read it out loud, and fill our houses with it. Deuteronomy 6:9 says we should write God's Word on our doorposts and gates. Remember all those verses we've been collecting? Why not put them on Post-its and stick them everywhere! Put them in the bathroom, the kitchen, each of the bedrooms, even the doorframes, and pray them whenever you pass by.

3. Pray on Location

A friend of mine shared this story with me:

> One night a number of years back, one of my children came into my room complaining of a

nightmare. He was scared and upset, so I comforted him and sent him back to bed. Within five minutes or so another child woke up and came to my room afraid. They'd had a nightmare too. I prayed for them, and they went back to bed. Twenty minutes later, my third child woke up, terrified over a nightmare she'd had. By this point, I woke up fully and realized it was a spiritual attack. I couldn't just stay in bed, pray, and send my kids back to bed. I got up, went into their rooms, and prayed over each of them and their bedrooms while they slept. I had to get out of my bed and go to the place of battle, to pray over them and over their rooms. Of course, they slept fine after that.

Though Jesus could have healed people from *any* location (as we see with the centurion in Matt. 8:5–13), He usually traveled to them. If your son is having trouble, pray in his room. If your whole house doesn't feel peaceful, walk around the perimeter of it while you pray. If your daughter is having trouble in school, pray while driving around the property. Praying on location strengthens our hearts' resolve and therefore increases the earnestness with which we pray.

4. Use Praise

After King Jehoshaphat and all Israel sought the Lord for help, God answered by saying:

Do not be afraid or discouraged because of this
vast number, for the battle is not yours, but God's.
Tomorrow, go down against them.... You do not
have to fight this battle. Position yourselves, stand
still, and see the salvation of the LORD.... Do not
be afraid or discouraged. Tomorrow, go out to
face them, for the LORD is with you. (2 Chron.
20:15b–17)

Because Jehoshaphat was full of joy at God's word, he went
ahead and "appointed men to sing to the LORD and to praise him
for the splendor of his holiness as they went out at the head of
the army, saying: 'Give thanks to the LORD, for his love endures
forever'" (v. 21 NIV).

As they marched forward, the worshippers took the front
lines. And it gets better. Verse 22 reads: "The *moment* they began
their shouts and praises, the LORD set an ambush against the
Ammonites, Moabites, and the inhabitants of Mount Seir who
came to fight against Judah, and they were defeated."

Did you catch that? "The moment they began their shouts and
praises" their enemies were defeated. Our worship is powerful; I
believe it affects the spiritual atmosphere of the spaces we worship
in. When we sing praise while walking around the rooms of our
homes or the neighborhoods we live in, it's as if we are pushing
back evil and claiming territory for God's kingdom.

A side note: I believe we can invite our children to pray with
us in these seasons; however, it may be helpful to stick to talking about the action we're taking rather than what we think the

cause of the problem may be. For instance, saying "I think Satan is attacking our house" may not only scare a child, but it may also be far from the truth. We might opt for something more like, "The Bible shows us that when we pray verses, it's like we're using a sword to fight against evil."

Children Will Respond Differently to Hardship

If you have more than one child, you know how different children are from one another. They express joy, as well as pain and frustration, in different ways. When I walked in the door with our new puppy, I received five very different reactions from our five children. One child lit up with total delight, just a giant smile. Another was shocked; her face froze in amazement and disbelief. "What?" one of my sons asked, confused as to why I was holding a dog and unsure of what was going on. While those three were taking it in, my second oldest daughter gasped and screamed instantly; then, knowing it wouldn't be appropriate for her to stand there screaming, ran around the house and came back. The youngest covered his little ears and cried because he didn't understand what was going on.

While it'd be fabulous if our children all embraced prayer in hard seasons, that simply may not be the case. We should not expect that there will be a one-size-fits-all solution. While some children may cling to family prayer, others may withdraw. While one child may thank God for His love, another may feel hurt and incredibly unloved by God. In these seasons, one-on-one prayer is going to be incredibly helpful because we can tailor those times with our children to their individual needs. As was the case with our puppy, no response is right or wrong; they are just different.

Sometimes our children want nothing to do with us or what we have to offer, even if that's God. I recently sat with a mother who expressed great sadness over her son's relationship with God. He refused to pray and was very resistant to anything having to do with God or church. Those times are so difficult. There are few things more heartbreaking to us as Christian parents than our children rejecting God. How can we bring them to Jesus if they refuse? Here are five practical steps to consider.

1. Try to determine the source of their resistance.

When my brother was young, he was incredibly moody and often grumpy for no apparent reason. Eventually, my parents discovered he had chronic ear infections. Because he was so accustomed to the pain, it never occurred to him that something was wrong. Treating his ears helped tremendously.

Sometimes when our kids push us away or refuse to pray or even talk about God, it's not indicative of their hearts or how we're doing as parents. There could be a number of situational factors: their mood, comprehension level, sickness, pain (e.g., an earache), emotional capacity, age, hunger level, energy level, and so on. If your five-year-old yells, "I don't want to pray, and I *don't* want to talk to God either!" (yup, that just happened in our house), it is likely a result of one or more circumstantial and therefore temporary issues. More often than not, asking some questions and increasing the amount of one-on-one time we have with them will help tremendously.

2. Partner up with your spouse or a good friend.

If what you're experiencing with your child seems to be more than just circumstantial, talk with your spouse (or another trusted family member) about it. Decide right from the start to be on the same page. Commit to praying about your son or daughter together, and maybe choose a few days to fast together as well. If appropriate, invite a sibling or two to join you in committing to pray.

3. Connect them with resources to help them grow.

Around ten years of age, my one daughter was pretty cold whenever I tried to talk about God. There were several factors that contributed to this, but we saw a change after I provided some age-appropriate resources for her to read at her leisure. It turns out it was incredibly helpful for her to pursue her faith on her own, as opposed to when we brought it up.

Assess the materials available to your children. Do they have an age-appropriate Bible? Are there some Christian programs, shows, books, a youth or kids group, a monthly magazine, or even a conference that will speak to their age and interest level? If not, now is a great time to introduce them to creative resources that will allow them to seek God on their own.

4. Wait for the open door; don't pry it open.

We need lots of discernment to determine whether our efforts are helping or hurting. Sometimes approaching a resistant child will cause them to recoil and withdraw even more. If their door is closed, then let it be closed, and don't try to pry it open. Our job at that point is to pray and wait for an open door. Then, when the door opens, we can be ready. If a pet dies or they are having trouble with a friend, that may be an open door. That might be an opportunity to come alongside them and say, "I'm so sorry. Do you want to pray about this together?"

5. Reset your parent-child relationship.

If there is a rift in your relationship with your child, go back to the basics. Show that you care about them and your relationship. Get on their level and revisit their interests. Pursue them in ways that are meaningful to *them*.

When my brother was in middle school, my parents became frustrated with his behavior. He resisted his chores and was disrespectful, and his relationship with our dad was strained. Thankfully, my parents received some sage advice, made a plan, and ran with it. My mom decided to handle enforcing chores and homework, while my father focused on relationship building. He put more time and energy into doing fun things and bonding over my brother's interests. My brother turned around. I doubt if he jumped at the chance to do his chores, but he developed a much better relationship with my parents and was able to do some fun things in the process.

The reality is, no matter how intentional we are, we do not control our children's faith. We cannot save them or make them have a relationship with Jesus. As we've said from the beginning, our role is simply to bring them to Jesus, like the people did in Matthew 19. If they continue to be resistant or refuse, we can continue to pray for them, and we can partner with our spouses and intercede on their behalf. One of the hardest prayers I've ever prayed is "Lord, do whatever it takes to bring my children to You." While we'd never wish hardship on our children, sometimes— just like He did with Manasseh (not that any of our children are wicked and awful like he was!)—God will use adversity to bring lost ones to their knees.

 The reality is, no matter how intentional we are, we do not control our children's faith.

The Larger Body of Christ

Speaking of her daughter, a friend once asked, "Can you tell her? She'll receive it better if it comes from you." I was surprised by my friend's words but refrained from blurting out, "Yeah, but you're her *mom*!" While there *is* a special role that we as parents play in discipling our children, the body of Christ plays a special role as well. Even though it may be our instinct to withdraw, we need each other, and we especially need the body of Christ.

The various parts of the body work together to accomplish amazing things. We will prevent ourselves and our children from experiencing a whole host of blessings if we neglect to reach out to others, especially in times of need. Perhaps now is a good time to reach out to others, such as a small group, a trusted youth group leader, a friend, or a grandparent.

If you have entered a particularly difficult season, the church as an *organization* may not have the therapy program or small group that you need. Turning to the body of Christ in an intense season may primarily look like turning to just one or two mentors. They might not have experienced what you have, but they will answer when you call, they will pray when you cry, and they will pick you up when you fall. If you're in that season now, seek a trusted individual who can be there for you.

Cereal Is Acceptable Dinner

In hard seasons, time and mental space are a luxury. In order to lean into God and have any capacity to meet with our children, we'll need to give ourselves a lot more grace and let go of some things.

After moving to New York, I gradually became acquainted with our neighbors and was thrilled to discover another Christian woman on the block. Not only did she have four children who were about the same ages as mine, she also homeschooled them. Naturally, we became great friends. I was regularly amazed by her endless energy. She was doing lots of activities with her children, eating healthy, reading her Bible regularly, and—wait for it—she even worked out *daily*! She was busy but also excellent at prioritizing. Could she get any better?

On occasion, her husband was either away or had to work late and couldn't help with the evening schedule. After telling me all she had to manage the evening before, I said, "How did you have time to make dinner?" With zero hesitation or shame she said, "Oh, they all had cereal." "Really?" I couldn't believe it. But then it got more surprising. "Yeah, they have cereal for dinner whenever it's really busy. They love it." What?! This wasn't just a one-time desperate move? It's, like, a *thing*? Here was my do-it-all, healthy, workout friend who fed her children cereal for dinner—not just once but on *multiple* occasions. Any pride I felt in discovering my friend didn't do everything perfectly was quickly plowed over by a profound sense of freedom. I had never considered cereal an option for dinner. I didn't even know it was allowed!

Striving to be good parents can often leave us feeling like we're juggling our children, activities, and marriages with the sense that if we mess up, everything may fall. One wrong step might mean disaster. Yet, our God is *full* of grace. Colossians 1:17 says that Jesus "is before all things, and by him all things hold together." Do you know what that grace means for us in hard times? That means that cereal is acceptable for dinner.

I recently felt so exhausted and discouraged. While everyone grabbed a seat in the family room for devotions, I sat back in the rocking chair, knowing I had nothing in me to give. Normally, we would have pulled out a book and a few Bibles to get started. I don't know if my husband picked up on my exhaustion or was distracted, but he grabbed his guitar down from the wall, dug around in his pocket for a pick, and began strumming. I just sat. It was as if his strumming brought the comfort of God into the room like a warm weighted blanket. The kids also just sat, and we all listened.

We may need to let go of our agendas and expectations and just be with God in the simplest of ways. If you're in the middle of a trying season, what might "cereal for dinner" look like for you? We've no need to make things look a certain way; we only need to look in a certain direction—to God.

A Final Word

This testimony comes from the friend I mentioned at the beginning of this chapter who had a suicidal and abusive husband:

> Nothing seemed certain. My husband had threatened us again, and my biggest concern was how I was going to provide for our children. While I was in one of my children's rooms, praying again, I heard the audible voice of God. I literally heard Him. He said, "I will provide for them." We went through many more years of hardship, but I never once doubted God would provide because He said He would.

Did you notice that God didn't say anything to King Jehoshaphat about sending worshippers to the front lines? God actually told him that everyone should take their positions and stand firm. Jehoshaphat led his soldiers with praise and joy because he had *complete confidence* in God's words! He was like a wimpy kid bringing his beefy big brother to the playground to face the bully who threatened him the day before. Instead of cowering as he had in the past, he strutted out, chipperly whistling away.

My friend's words remind me that we can count on God like no one else. He holds everything together, and He is big enough to carry even our heaviest burdens and fight our greatest enemies. When we're in a battle, we can rest assured and even praise God with confidence, knowing He's got our back!

As we bring our children to God in prayer, they will see over and over that God is trustworthy. In hard times especially, they will see for *themselves* that He is who He says He is! Every storm we experience will only lead us to know God and His power more. And after experiencing God's shelter, comfort, and deliverance, our children will know who to praise when the storm is over!

Chapter 12

A LEGACY OF ETERNAL VALUE

If my house were burning down and my children were safely outside, I know exactly which item I would want to grab. Surely, I'm not the only one who lies awake at night thinking these things through!

The *one thing* I would grab is the shoebox that sits under the foot of our bed. It has the word *ARk* written on it in Sharpie. Just like that. Capital *A*, capital *R*, lowercase *k*. There's no deep meaning for the odd capitalization. I accidentally started to write *Altar* instead of *Ark*, so the *l* from *Altar* became an uppercase *R*. Despite its name, the shoebox looks terribly ordinary.

As you might have guessed, the box is named after the ark of the covenant that God instructed Moses to build in the book of Exodus. Unlike my cardboard box, that ark was ornate and impressive. It was built from acacia wood, overlaid inside and out with gold, and had two gold cherubim sitting on top.

Captivating, I'm sure. But as magnificent as the outside looked, the real treasure was within the ark. No, not jewels or precious metals. The ark contained two rocks, a wooden stick, and bread. Doesn't that sound impressive?

But here's why they were: each of those objects represented the hand of God at work among His people. The two rocks were the stone tablets that God Himself wrote the Ten Commandments on, and the wooden stick was Aaron's staff that budded, blossomed, and produced almonds as a sign that showed who the priests would be. And the bread was the manna that God miraculously provided for the Israelites to eat while they were in the desert.

Each of these objects was kept so the Israelite people would always have the testimony of God before them. The ark of the covenant is sometimes referred to by another name: the ark of the testimony. The objects inside symbolized God's covenant with His people, but they also functioned as the proof, or a testimony. They were a reminder of God's faithfulness to that covenant.

Though my shoebox doesn't contain anything quite as spectacular as the original ark, it holds the same sentiment. Our ordinary yet precious box is packed with slips of paper, note cards, and Post-its, each one with a story, a testimony of God's hand at work in our lives.

Some events are casual but meaningful blessings from the Lord. Like the time I wanted so badly to throw a party for my daughter but we had zero extra cash. However, the night before her birthday, I received a call from a friend saying they had a ton of leftover food from a large family get-together and wondered if we wanted to all have lunch together after church the next day. Then before church the following morning, a different friend said she had baked cupcakes for an event but made a mistake and had a bunch left over. Our family and friends got together after church and joyfully celebrated my daughter's birthday. Not only did we have food for the meal, but we had dessert too! It was a party thrown by God.

Other stories are harder to explain. Like the time my husband pleaded with Jesus to heal my son from anaphylactic shock, and he went from unresponsive to alert at the name of Jesus. Or the time I received a call from an acquaintance. She told me that while she was driving that morning, she kept hearing the phrase "I know the plans I have for you." She assumed it was for her until she saw a mental picture of my family standing together in a field of purple flowers. I hung up the phone thinking, *All right, that's cool.* It wasn't until I told my husband that I understood how significant her call was because, in awe, he went on to tell me that all morning he had been praying, *Lord, I don't know what Your plans are, but please, just show me that You have plans.*

For the past fifteen years, my husband and I have made it a practice to pull out the box at least once a year, not only to remember all God has done but also to add new testimonies to the box. I have no priceless heirlooms or significant jewelry to grab if my house were burning down, but I believe the legacy contained in my shoebox is of greater value than anything I could own. Like the real ark, that shoebox represents the hand of God at work in our lives.

We started off this book with a goal to help our children know Jesus for themselves through prayer. Our confident hope is that as our children have more and more experiences with Jesus, they will develop a rich history with God. And this history will serve to cultivate a trust in God that, like the roots of the tree from Jeremiah 17, will sustain them through the many seasons and storms of life.

Throughout these chapters, we've learned how to bring our children to Jesus. We've learned how to come alongside them and guide them in prayer. From those chubby little toddler hands folded at the dinner table through the middle school years— where they've not only prayed with us but have also had a plethora of their own prayer experiences—they've begun to develop their own prayer practices and routines.

So we've just one more thing to discuss—*keeping the testimony*. We want to ensure their history with God is not forgotten. We don't want these events, their growth, or *any* move of God to be ignored. They will not remember those early prayers, nor the way God answered them, but *we* can. They may not see the significance of various events, but *we* will. They will not have the perspective to see that in the really hard season they actually grew the most, but *we* do.

All these experiences are part of the testimony of God's hand at work. We keep the testimony when we remember—and retell— what He has done.

 When we share with our children what God *has* done, it sparks their faith for what He *will* do.

Testimonies are stories from the past that inform our faith for the future. I can't think of a single thing that encourages my faith more than a powerful story of God's work in someone's life. When we share with our children what God *has* done, it sparks their faith for what He *will* do. God wants us to know that the God who did *x*, *y*, and *z* in the past is the *same* God who is with us now. Keeping the testimony, therefore, is not just remembering and retelling, but living in the present reality and future hope that God, in all His fullness, is here now and won't leave.

I had previously avoided telling my daughter about the time I put her in her infant car seat but forgot to put her seat in the car before pulling out of my parking spot. Thankfully, a nearby woman waved frantically and yelled to get my attention. Talk about embarrassing! "Oh yes, you know what? That *is* my baby, thank you." I don't think I could've hung my head any lower.

Thirteen years later I did tell her what happened. I admitted that I hadn't told her before because I was so embarrassed by it, but then I realized she needed to know because it was part of her testimony. Immediately after it happened, I praised God for the woman in the parking lot that night and wondered if she was an angel! God protected my baby that night, and no matter how embarrassing it was for me, that is part of His work in my daughter's life. And, therefore, it's something worth remembering.

Now, she carries that testimony. Like the ark that was always before the Israelites, this little story is now one more bit of history she has with God. It's just another piece of assurance that she serves an active and loving God. It's one more story to increase her trust in Him. Just as trees grow a new ring each year, our children's experiences with God over time will serve to strengthen and grow them.

The Role Parents Play

We as parents play a unique and crucial role in remembering God's work. Did you know that God condemned the Israelites for not remembering the law, yet several times the book of the law (the only documentation of the law) went missing? Not to mention, the majority of people at that time couldn't read.

If there was no book to read and the firsthand witnesses were long gone, who do you think bore the responsibility to remember? The parents! One might think the leaders, priests, and kings had the job of remembering—and they certainly had a role to play— but no one else was specifically tasked to remember the way God called parents to.

> I may do these miraculous signs of mine among them,... so that you may tell your son and grandson. (Ex. 10:1b–2a)

> Understand today that it is not your children who experienced or saw the discipline of the LORD your God: His greatness, strong hand, and outstretched arm.... Teach them to your children, talking about them when you sit in your house and when you walk along the road, when you lie down and when you get up. (Deut. 11:2, 19)

Before cell phones, the internet, cameras, encyclopedias, and a high literacy rate, information was primarily passed on from parent to child. A beautiful image comes to mind of generation after generation passing on the works of the Lord, as Joel describes:

> Has anything like this ever happened in
>   your days
> or in the days of your ancestors?
> Tell your children about it,
> and let your children tell their children,
> and their children the next generation.
> (Joel 1:2b–3)

When we step back to understand the big picture of the message here, we see that we are not only responsible for remembering what God does in our children's lives but also for telling our children what He did *before* they were born. Our children's history with God doesn't actually begin with their chubby hands folded at the table for the first time. It begins long before that. When we bring our children to Jesus, we are actually bringing them to a foundation that was developing before they were even born.

I was recently asked to share my testimony of coming to know Christ. I started with the day my mother received Christ over the phone after calling a 1-800 number. (True story!) But I could have just as easily begun with the time my father put his faith in Jesus as a teenager because of a special mentor in his life. Or the occasion where two Gideons gave my grandmother her first Bible when she was just a little girl. Each of these events

happened well before I was born, but they are a part of the testimony I carry.

What God has done in our day is meant to be passed on to
our children. It's not just for us; it's an inheritance for them as
well. What has God done in your life, maybe even before you
were born? What prayers has He answered? What storms has He
calmed? What mountains has He moved? In what ways has He
provided for you?

Even if you don't have much of a personal or family history
with Jesus, you still have a foundation. An ancient one in fact.
Have you ever reflected on the fact that hundreds of years *after*
God parted the Red Sea, He chided the Israelites for forgetting
about it?

Imagine a teacher giving you an F because you couldn't
remember an event that you weren't alive for and there was no
documentation of. Yet that's exactly what God did. God expected
His people to remember what He had done for them, whether they
had *personally* experienced it or not. He wanted them to hold on
to that miracle as if it were *their* lives that were spared and *their*
feet that walked on dry ground and *their* eyes that saw a wall of
water to their left and a wall of water to their right.

When we become members of God's family, we inherit a long,
rich, and powerful history of God loving His people. Consider the
following passage from Ephesians:

> You are no longer foreigners and strangers, but
> *fellow citizens* with the saints, and *members* of
> God's household, built on the foundation of the

apostles and prophets, with Christ Jesus himself as
the cornerstone. In him the whole building, being
put together, grows into a holy temple in the Lord.
(2:19–21)

Hopefully, you're sitting there reading and thinking, *This is
great. Yes, I want to remember what God has done. I want to keep
the testimony of His work so I can pass it on to my children!* If you
are, then bravo! I'm so glad. There's just one little problem—you
are prone to forgetting. I am prone to forgetting. We as humans
are forgetful by nature.

We Will Forget Unless We *Actively* Remember

Let's face it, we all forget. Even our family's tooth fairy is forgetful.
Now, the kids just put their teeth under *my* pillow! I can't tell you
how many times I've thought to myself, *I wish I could remember
this moment forever!* Yet, no matter how important something
is at the time, it doesn't mean we *will* remember it. This is true
whether we're talking about events, relationships, information,
conversations, feelings, our children, and even God.

Thankfully, God knows how easy it is for us to forget. Like us,
the Israelites were forgetful too. This is why, alongside God's commands to remember, God provided *ways* to help them remember.
He instructed people to build altars and cairns as physical signs
and ways to remember what He had done. He assigned annual
feasts and fasts to serve as a remembrance. Consider the words
spoken about Purim:

> These days are remembered and celebrated by
> every generation, family, province, and city, so
> that these days of Purim will not lose their signifi-
> cance in Jewish life and their *memory will not fade
> from their descendants*. (Est. 9:28)

Did you know that God even commanded special clothing to be worn? Down to the tassels, the details of the priests' garments were symbols to help the people remember (see Num. 15:39). Even when Jesus celebrated Passover with His disciples and told them to remember the new covenant, He gave them a symbol to aid in their remembrance—one that we still reenact today. When we break bread and share wine together, we remember Jesus.

> After supper he took the cup, saying, "This cup
> is the new covenant in my blood; do this, when-
> ever you drink it, in *remembrance* of me." (1 Cor.
> 11:25 NIV)

In order to look back on the work God has done in our own lives and be able to pass it on to our children, we too need some actions to help us remember. I once heard about a woman who kept a small rock for every time God answered a prayer. Throughout her house, you could see small rocks placed as mementos to God's work in her life.

Let's take a look at some ways we can fight our human ten-dency to forget.

Talk about it. This is the simplest. When something significant happens, a small blessing, an answered prayer, a good day—talk about it. Share it with your children, your spouse, your friends. Discuss it when you're walking around the block or recounting the day before bed. When we string words together into sentences and organize sentences to tell a story, the memory becomes more concrete in our minds. Having a conversation about an event will not only help us remember the event, but it is also how we pass it on to our children.

Write it down. Our brains may forget, but our paper won't. This is why I treasure my "ARk" box. I can easily refer to it whenever I want. For several years, I wrote significant events on our family calendar, not just birthdays and anniversaries but also when a prayer was answered, when God met us in a special way, when He did something significant, and the like. Each new year I carried those events over to the new calendar.

Remember that journal you gave your child? When something special happens, tell them to record it there so they never forget. Or maybe you want to start an "ark" as a family. However we choose to record things, it is incredibly important to do so.

Celebrate holidays. Holidays can be a perfect opportunity to remember significant events or make note of recent ones. For several years, we decorated our Christmas tree with paper ornaments that had the kids' favorite memories from the year written on them.

Like Purim, all the biblical holidays were meant to be a time of remembrance and have deep meaning attached to them. Don't get distracted by the secular meaning that gets tangled into our holidays. Revisit and remember the real meaning and deeper truths behind the days we celebrate. How might your family intentionally incorporate remembering into the holidays and special occasions you celebrate?

Remember birthdays. These are my favorite occasions to remember. Consider having a time of storytelling on your child's birthday—about their birth or adoption, the meaning behind their name, significant memories, or moments of growth.

There's Eternal Work to Be Done

After a dramatic exit from Egypt and forty long years in the desert, God brought the Israelites right to the edge of the Promised Land. Decades of nomadic tent life were almost over; they were finally going to settle, build homes, and plow fields.

There was a catch though. Before the Israelites could settle into the land, they had to fight the people who were living there and drive them out. This must have felt like a giant déjà vu for Moses, because forty years prior, the previous generation had had this same opportunity but, sadly, didn't take it.

Moses had sent twelve men to scope out the land and spy on those living there. But after observing the city and men who lived there, they were too afraid to fight. "We can't attack the people because they are stronger than we are!" (Num. 13:31). The consequences of their disobedience affected the entire nation of Israel. God issued a punishment for their lack of faith: they were to wander the desert for forty years.

In that time, one by one, that generation of parents passed away in the lifeless desert. Can you imagine the regret they must have felt? Because *they* lacked faith, instead of feeding their children milk and honey, they tasted the bitterness of a barren land for forty years. Instead of their children inheriting homes, wells, and vineyards, they inherited sand and, worse, the inevitability of war. The work that was assigned to the first generation got passed off to their children.

This time, forty years later, Moses brought the Israelites to the edge of the Promised Land once again. All but two people from the original generation had died, and those who had been children were now grown. And for a second time, the Israelites had the chance to enter the Promised Land by conquering the peoples who lived there.

I imagine that any reservations the men had about going into battle were quickly squashed by remembering the bitterness of their parents' cowardice. *I'm not just doing this for me. I'm fighting so my children won't have to. This is for my children, my grandchildren, and all my descendants!*

As with the first generation of Israelites, our own lack of faith and limited perspective can keep us from doing hard things. We too are prone to think of ourselves, our preferences, and what's most convenient right now.

But—lean in a little—there is eternal work to be done.

 When you get weary because your children are being rowdy and don't seem to care, remember the work of prayer is *eternal*.

The Israelites were afraid and intimidated by their enemy. I doubt that we're afraid of our enemy, but not for good reasons. If I'm being honest, I'm usually just in denial that there is one! But he's around. Satan is actively fighting against God, prowling like a lion and seeking ones to destroy. There is a war going on, and our prayers are fueling God's plans, kingdom, and purpose by pushing back the darkness until the time when Satan is cast down forever. We are not just teaching our children how to pray, as if praying were a passive action; we are teaching them how to battle. We are inviting our children to be active and discerning members of God's kingdom.

The children of the first generation did the work to defeat their enemies. They were able to settle in the beautiful and luscious land. And guess what. It wasn't just for them and their children. It was for their children's children's children's children's children's ... Goodness, descendants are living there today!

When you get weary because your children are being rowdy and don't seem to care, remember the work of prayer is *eternal*. Don't let discouragement sidetrack you. Prayer is not just for your children; it's for all who come after. There is work to be done *now*, and we have no idea how it'll impact our children's futures. But we can be confident it absolutely will.

> From eternity to eternity
> the LORD's faithful love is toward those who
> fear him,
> and his righteousness toward the grandchildren
> of those who keep his covenant,
> who remember to observe his precepts.
> (Ps. 103:17–18)

Let's do the work of bringing our children to Jesus in prayer. Let's make prayer a beautiful and foundational part of our home. Let's be creative with prayer so our children experience many different ways to engage with God. Let's sit on the edge of their beds and pray with them even when there's a hundred other things we could be doing, because we know the lasting impact of the Lord's work.

Let's do the work.

Two Temples

A Builder builded a temple,
He wrought it with grace and skill;
Pillars and groins and arches
All fashioned to work his will.
Men said, as they saw its beauty,
"It shall never know decay;
Great is thy skill, O Builder!
Thy fame shall endure for aye."

A Mother builded a temple
With loving and infinite care,
Planning each arch with patience,
Laying each stone with prayer.
None praised her unceasing efforts,
None knew of her wondrous plan,
For the temple the Mother builded
Was unseen by the eyes of man.

Gone is the Builder's temple,
Crumpled into the dust;
Low lies each stately pillar,
Food for consuming rust.
But the temple the Mother builded
Will last while the ages roll,
For that beautiful unseen temple
Was a child's immortal soul.

Hattie Vose Hall[1]

Imagine the joy here on earth when we see our children and grandchildren come to know Jesus, when we see others healed because of their prayers, when we see lives changed through their intercession. And more than that, imagine the joy we will experience someday with Christ when we clearly see *all* the fruit of our prayers that we never saw on earth! Our work in Christ is the *only* work we'll be able to look back on and say, "Yes, *that* was worth it."

VERSES TO PRAY

"Love the Lord your God with all your heart and with all your soul and with all your mind." This is the first and greatest commandment. And the second is like it: "Love your neighbor as yourself." All the Law and the Prophets hang on these two commandments. (Matt. 22:37–40 NIV)

Seek first his kingdom and his righteousness, and all these things will be given to you as well. (Matt. 6:33 NIV)

Trust in the LORD with all your heart and lean not on your own understanding; in all your ways submit to him, and he will make your paths straight. (Prov. 3:5–6 NIV)

You will seek me and find me when you seek me with all your heart. (Jer. 29:13 NIV)

Whatever you did for the least of these brothers and sisters of mine, you did for me. (Matt. 25:40b NIV)

The one who stands firm to the end will be saved. (Matt. 24:13 NIV)

Watch and pray so that you will not fall into temptation. The spirit is willing, but the flesh is weak. (Matt. 26:41 NIV)

I have told you these things, so that in me you may have peace. In this world you will have trouble. But take heart! I have overcome the world. (John 16:33 NIV)

Be strong and courageous. Do not be afraid or terrified because of them, for the LORD your God goes with you; he will never leave you nor forsake you. (Deut. 31:6 NIV)

Samuel said, "Speak, for your servant is listening." (1 Sam. 3:10 NIV)

May these words of my mouth and this meditation of my heart be pleasing in your sight, LORD, my Rock and my Redeemer. (Ps. 19:14 NIV)

Set a guard over my mouth, LORD; keep watch over the door of my lips. (Ps. 141:3 NIV)

"Not by might nor by power, but by my Spirit," says the LORD Almighty. (Zech. 4:6 NIV)

Show me your ways, LORD, teach me your paths. (Ps. 25:4 NIV)

You are good, and what you do is good; teach me your decrees. (Ps. 119:68 NIV)

I will give them singleness of heart and action, so that they will always fear me and that all will then go well for them and for their children after them. (Jer. 32:39 NIV)

My covenant was with him, a covenant of life and peace, and I gave them to him; this called for reverence and he revered me and stood in awe of my name. (Mal. 2:5 NIV)

He did what was right in the eyes of the LORD and followed completely the ways of his father David, not turning aside to the right or to the left. (2 Kings 22:2 NIV)

Whether you turn to the right or to the left, your ears will hear a voice behind you, saying, "This is the way; walk in it." (Isa. 30:21 NIV)

NOTES

Chapter 1: The Greatest Inheritance

1. "Parents Describe How They Raise Their Children," Barna Group, February 28, 2005, www.barna.com/research/parents-describe-how-they-raise-their -children.

Chapter 2: Maybe They'll Get It When They're Older

1. "Child Trafficking: Myth vs. Fact," Save the Children, accessed October 26, 2022, www.savethechildren.org/us/charity-stories/child-trafficking-myth s-vs-facts#:~:text=Trafficking%3A%20Myth%20vs.-,Fact,victims%20are %20girls%5Bi%5D.

2. Donna St. George, "School Shootings Rose to Highest Number in 20 Years, Federal Data Says," *Washington Post*, June 28, 2022, www.washingtonpost .com/education/2022/06/28/school-shootings-crime-report.

3. Oxford Languages Dictionary as quoted by Google, accessed October 26, 2022, www.google.com/search?q=definitions+of+expert&oq=definitions+of +expert&aqs=chrome..69i57j0i10i15i22i30j0i22i30l8.2735j0j15&sourceid =chrome&ie=UTF-8.

4. *Alone*, "Pins and Needles," History Channel video, 42:50, 2020, https://play.history.com/shows/alone/season-7/episode-10.

Chapter 7: What Prayer Can Look Like

1. "Pope Francis' Five Finger Prayer," Holy Cross Catholic Parish, accessed August 11, 2022, https://hcpsb.org/parish-information/prayer-line/pope -francis-five-finger-prayer.

Chapter 12: A Legacy of Eternal Value

1. Hattie Vose Hall, "Two Temples," in *The Best Loved Poems of the American People* (New York: Doubleday, 1936), 392.

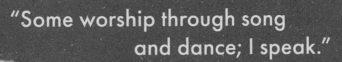

"Some worship through song
and dance; I speak."
—Erica Renaud

Want to equip families in your congregation to pray with their children?

Invite Erica to teach on this topic in person. Praying with Children is a perfect seminar for parents, children's ministry leaders and volunteers. Attendees will leave inspired and ready to bring authentic and powerful prayer into their home or classroom!

Hosting an event?

Invite Erica to come speak! She loves to teach from the Word and speak about worship, prayer, motherhood, and homeschooling. She speaks at a variety of events including:

- Conferences
- Worship Events
- Panel Discussions

estherpress

Our journey invites us deeper into God's Word, where wisdom waits to renew our minds and where the Holy Spirit meets us in discernment that empowers bold action for such a time as this.

If we have the courage to say yes to our calling and no to everything else, will the world be ready?

JOIN US IN COURAGEOUS LIVING

Your Esther Press purchase helps to equip, encourage, and disciple women around the globe with practical assistance and spiritual mentoring to help them become strong leaders and faithful followers of Jesus.

An imprint of

DAVID C COOK

transforming lives together